The Warrior within You

A True Story That Makes NLP Simple, Understandable and Applicable in Real Life

notionpress.com

The Warrior Within You

A True Story That Makes NLP Simple, Understandable and Applicable in Real Life

Syed Habeeb

notionpress.com

Notion Press

Old No. 38, New No. 6

McNichols Road, Chetpet

Chennai - 600 031

First Published by Notion Press 2016

ISBN 978-93-5206-672-8

DEDICATED TO

The Almighty

Who has given us everything we have

and created beautiful laws and principles for us to

recognize, use and benefit for life.

"Life is similar to the sport of boxing.
Defeat is not declared when you fall down;
It is declared when you refuse to GET UP."

Contents

FOREWORD

The biggest room in this world is the room for self-development.

In an era where the newspaper looks more like a full-fledged magazine, a man who cannot afford his footwear can afford a flight ticket and the doctor installs a phone booth at his clinic as an extra source of income (yes, I have seen this), let us talk about the most important person in this universe: YOU.

In this incredibly chaotic materialistic world, which is short on values, how can we live to create a positive impact on our own life, our family, the people around us, our nation and the whole wide world at large?

What if you could achieve your true calling in life? What if you chose to tread a path and you didn't have a minute of regret? This is exactly what living legends and extraordinary people do. They do what they love all the time or love what they do, if forced by circumstances. When you ask them how they did it, their most probable answer would be an inspiring story that sparked the fire within, followed by focused and continuous modeling of outstanding people.

I am a very strong believer that every individual has been created with an unlimited reserve of power within. This power drives us to run towards something higher all the time. If we spend our time chasing mere material goals, we end up burning this power for almost nothing in return. So the bigger challenge in life is making the right decisions and not making mere choices of a few goals and dreams.

There is a greater dissatisfaction and disappointment with wrong decisions than the non-achievement of goals. We know many extraordinary people who have pursued seemingly mammoth goals that led them to fail again and again. However, they never experienced the emotion of being a failure ever. In fact, every time they went down, they worked harder and more passionately in their next attempt. The crazy part is, when asked about their experience, almost all of them said they had "an amazing time" or something similar.

The thoughts penned in the pages to come could be a source of much-awaited inspiration for you. I have consciously penned short and crisp chapters as I belong to the fast food gen. We love things fast and crisp and thoughts must be fast and crisp too. So be it, fast food for thought.' Any concept or story shared in this book has the potential to ignite the spark inside you and connect you to your true calling in life. This book is intended to share simple yet profound laws of thinking, organizing, deciding and executing. Once you reflect and make these key non-negotiable and irrevocable decisions, you will find the renewed fire within you which will guide you to choose and achieve meaningful outcomes.

You must acknowledge the fact that you are already special. Among the millions of species on earth, you have been chosen to be a human being, the highest and most advanced form of creation. What I am about to share with you will introduce you to the latent potential bestowed within you to create the true YOU. This will help you stand up for what is right, swim against the tide and unlock the warrior within you to achieve a more meaningful success that is exclusive and incomparable.

The success you experience may not necessarily measure up to the clichéd idea of success that common people desire in the routine rat race. But it will certainly be the kind of success you will cherish in the journey of your life. Once you achieve this state, you will have seamless access to excellence, happiness, contentment and the door that opens to a life in its true and magnificent form. I wish you the best of everything this wonderful life has to offer and invite you to explore the 'warrior' within you.

"If you don't stand for something, you are bound to fall for everything."

Stand tall and high, O miracle of life,
Before every fate ordained for you,
When the One who designs your destiny,
Calls you to pick your heart's desire.

- Syed Habeeb

The Making of this Book

Minds are like parachutes, they only function when they are open.

- Sir James Dewar

In the past decade of my journey in the area of self-development and self-actualization, I have met many thousands of people. Every child I saw was special, every teacher an inspiration, every parent unconditional and every soul a reflection of life on a colorful mirror. This is not a book about inspiring a caterpillar to become a better caterpillar but it is all about inspiring a caterpillar to transform into an extraordinary butterfly.

A winner is usually an outcome of the warrior within. Winning is the result and being a warrior causes this result. I have avoided the term 'winner' in my book as I believe an individual's success is attributed to the warrior attitude within him or her. It is a gut feeling deep down that urges us to take on impossible tasks and turn them around. That is what you and I did as an insignificant cell in our mother's womb. It was a race of millions of cells where you stood first, an absolute first. It was a race that didn't have a second place at all.

We are unconsciously equipped to survive, but we need conscious efforts to live. We are already warriors of sorts; we just need to harness the right attitude to recreate the magic of living. This book is about the warrior within us waiting to be unleashed.

Life skill and leadership skill development programs focus on those elements of change that require transformation in thinking, beliefs and behavior. Over the last decade, I have been blessed to be a part of many teams that work passionately for the betterment of the human potential. The tools and strategies taught in these programs have turned around many lives. The stories and incidents shared in the training sessions have inspired many people to do things they normally would not dare to attempt.

The feedback and inspiring words from the participants of these programs and their encouraging response motivated me to pen this book. So a large part of the credit for this book goes to all the individuals and life skill teams I have worked with.

This book is a narrative extracted from a true story. Some of the best learning comes from real life experiences. Though I have included the wisdom, concepts and thoughts of living legends, I have tried to map them to the character's journey. I have a very important note for you at the end of this book. You may not be able to get this message if you turn over to the last page now. There is no one right method to read a book. Some people read books right till the end in one sitting or in one day. Others read a few pages a day and there are some who read a page a day. In the following paragraphs, I have shared a few of my thoughts on how you can get the best of this book.

Read this: **LIFEISNOWHERE**.

A majority of people, in all probability, read this phrase as LIFE IS NOWHERE. The words intended are LIFE IS NOW HERE. This simply proves that human beings, by nature, identify the lesser important things in life with relative ease.

The hidden and more useful diamonds of life are usually missed out as ordinary stones. You can discover the diamonds if you focus on the finer details embedded in this book.

There are two ways you can read this book. You can read it like an observer who watches a plane take off; this gives momentary thrills but no sustainable feeling. This is how most people read even bestsellers. The moment they understand a concept, strategy or tool, they immediately relate it to somebody they know who needs it. The usual thoughts are: *this concept is a must for my dad, I hope I can help my wife change her behavior through this explanation, now I am convinced that my husband is a great mistake or my boss must read this book.* In this process, readers tend to forget the most important person in their lives: themselves. The second and more empowering way to read this (or any) book is to be the racer in a Formula 1 car and not the audience. Be the player on the field and not the referee. Be the enthusiast on the roller coaster ride and not the passerby. Get into the cockpit and take off, because that is where the action and juice is.

JUICE THIS BOOK

A man who does not read is no better than a man who cannot read.

- Mark Twain

Read this book as if it was written just for you. When you get into the shoes of the key character, you can experience the character's feelings and his breathtaking eureka moments. You can relate everything to the vivid range of emotions and challenges you faced and the choices you made in your life. You may discover many keys to unlock your hidden talent, fire up your latent potential and uncover the tools to fine-tune your strengths. You may also come across one sentence or incident that can bring about a profound shift in the direction of your life. This book can be a source of discovering what is already designed in your destiny. You can learn proven and endorsed strategies that help you overcome the challenges you are facing and are likely to face. And finally, you will have the opportunity to shape beliefs and values that living legends and outstanding achievers in history cultivated during their life, making them true warriors within. These answers, keys, tools, strategies, beliefs and values, if followed in the right manner, can catapult you from who you are to who you may not even have dreamt of.

So fasten your seat belts and experience the warrior within you.

Books are the bees which carry the quickening pollen from one to another mind.

- James Russell Lowell

NOTE: References to 'man', 'he', 'himself' or 'his' in this book apply obviously to both men and women.

Chapter 1

THE DARK NIGHT

Two roads diverged in a wood, and I took the one less traveled by. And that has made all the difference.

- Robert Frost

Hatim was walking with his head down, taking lazy and sloppy steps. It was a dark and chilly night in the month of April, in the early nineties. Not even one thought that crossed his mind was stable; a rush of mixed emotions bombarded his head. He felt an excruciating pain in his right wrist, with which he had slammed the main door of his house. He was still not sure if what he had done that evening was even remotely close to right, but he was certain it was not good. He checked his pockets and felt a few coins jingling. He counted them; they totaled seventy paisa (0.70 of a rupee). This wouldn't buy him even half a ticket to the next bus stop. Having no choice, he walked.

As he walked to nowhere, flashes of what had transpired over the past few years rushed into his mind. Hatim was from a middle-class family; he was the eldest of three children. His parents had struggled to provide him even formal schooling. Somehow he managed to study and he was about to complete his graduation in engineering. He was eager to explore his dreams in the world. Hatim was ambitious and ready to do whatever it took to make it big.

Hatim wanted to reach for the stars and was not ready to compromise his dreams for anything. But he was clueless about how he would convert his dreams to reality. As he approached the final lap, his father was a bit too hard on Hatim's choice of friends and the amount of time he spent with them.

Hatim's father was a very hardworking and aggressive man. He dictated every decision at home and the family had no option but to obey him. While Hatim envisioned being an entrepreneur, his father had other aspirations for him. "Complete your degree and get a job in the Gulf" was his slogan. But Hatim had already started planning a small part-time business with a few friends as partners. Hatim had obeyed his father's dictates all his life but now he was in no mood to sacrifice his dreams. Hatim started questioning whatever his father ordered him to do. A verbal battle commenced and it grew into a war. Though Hatim tried to explain to his father that his friends were neither dumb nor bookish but were street-smart, his father wouldn't listen. Hatim tried to explain that his friends had supported him with books, notes and revisions that were so essential to his upcoming final exams. But his father always thought that his friends were a big waste of time.

There was a loss of trust between father and son and all their conversations ended in a showdown. They had been at loggerheads with each other for a few years and the situation blew up on the dark night.

Hatim knocked on the main door of his house late at night and was greeted by a flurry of abuses from his father. Hatim reacted angrily and shouted back. Then his father declared that if Hatim wanted to stay in the house, he had to do it his way else he was free to take the highway. Without a second thought, Hatim opted for the highway.

It was a dark night indeed. At least for Hatim and his family. Hatim's mother cried uncontrollably and his sister was terrified. All the wrong thoughts crossed his sister's mind. The recent suicide cases in the neighborhood frightened her; she prayed that her brother didn't do anything like that. Hatim's younger brother was in the hostel and was not informed of the showdown at home.

The night was destined to be the longest night that Hatim would ever experience. He walked aimlessly, contemplating whether he had made a huge mistake by walking out. He wondered if he should get back home as he was the oldest of the three children and a lot depended on him. As he crossed the main crossroads, a sense of uncertainty mixed with fear haunted him. Where would he go?

Hatim wondered if he should get back and apologize to his father and continue tolerating the torture. "But why should I do that; it is no fault of mine," his inner voice told him. As thoughts made sinusoidal waves in his mind, he heard a familiar rattling sound behind. He turned around and was pleasantly surprised to see his close friend Chandy on his old bike. "What the hell are you doing walking here at this odd hour?" Chandy shouted. Hatim narrated the entire incident to him while they rode to the tea joint they frequented. Chandy advised Hatim to think again before he took any drastic step and ruined whatever little he had. The tea somehow seemed to help Hatim organize his thoughts. Finally, he was clear in his mind and said, "I will go back home, but only after I have proven to my dad that I can achieve what I believe in. I have no clue how I am going to prove myself, but I need to make it big for the sweat my parents have invested in me. I want to ensure my sister is well-settled and my brother gets a good mainstream education. Only then will God be pleased with me."

Hatim then broke down uncontrollably. He said, "I don't have any good feelings towards my dad anymore. It is just that we are made of completely different soil. Nothing is ever agreeable between us. I can't explain my dreams in words to him. I must prove myself through my actions. I am sure with time he will appreciate who I am and how grossly wrong he was."

Chandy rode for over eleven kilometers to a friend's place where they stayed overnight. Those were the days when mobile phones were not heard of. Hatim called home from a phone booth and assured his mother that he was fine and that he would come back when the time was right.

Hatim had to work extra hard as time was running faster than he could. He borrowed money from his friend and bought some clothes. He scouted for a decent paying guest accommodation and luckily got one quickly. His ambition grew stronger with each passing day. Routine took over and the days flew by and turned into months. Fear, uncertainty and desperation filled the air. Soon exams were around the corner. While his classmates viewed exams like monsters, they didn't haunt Hatim. Strangely, exams did not bother him anymore. In fact, he did not change his routine to accommodate a few extra hours for studying. He continued running the small business he had started with his friends. Exams were no more a goal for him, they were merely stepping stones to his real goals in life. He was crystal clear about what he wanted but he had absolutely no idea how he would get there. Every now and then, his gut feeling kept shouting to him, "I know where I want to go. I don't know how I will get there, but I want to get there."

Chapter 2

THE DAY AFTER YESTERDAY

Being defeated is often a temporary condition. Giving up is what makes it permanent.

- Marilyn Vos Savant

It was the summer of the mid-nineties. Hatim's final year results were out. There was total chaos in the college around the notice board where the results were listed. There was no internet those days. One had to go to the college and experience the emotions real time. Laughter, happiness, screaming and tears marked the day.

Hatim did not go to college that morning. All his friends were looking for him. Many of them called him on his feebly audible land phone, but he did not answer their calls. Eventually, the excitement and thrill subsided in a few hours and the college campus was deserted again.

That afternoon, Hatim had a sumptuous lunch and took a long walk to the college. Other than the security guard, who gave him a questioning stare, there was not a soul in the quadrangle. As Hatim walked up to the notice board, he looked down and felt his heart. The beats were normal and there was no change in his emotions. There was no sign of excitement or fear as he was absolutely confident that he had done well. There was no reason for him to think otherwise. As he ran his fingers down the mark list, he checked for EDB179, his hall ticket number. In fact, he was looking for just 179.

He ran through the distinction list and the first class list. His number wasn't to be seen. A mild cold feeling crept down his spine and his throat dried up. He quickly scanned the lists again. Hastily, he scanned the second class list; his number was not there too. In the next few minutes, it was evident to him that his number wasn't present anywhere on the board. Panting, he ran towards the office where the office bearer Lawrence was pulling out prints. He looked at Hatim a bit puzzled.

"Yes, what can I do?" Lawrence asked him. Hatim explained his problem and Lawrence pulled out the master register that had all the information related to the results. He pushed the register towards Hatim as though he already knew the results and there was no good news to share.

Hatim browsed to the bottom of the register and found two numbers that stood out – 179 and 176, both under the category 'detained.' The mild cold feeling in his spine grew into a warm rush around his neck and head. "This is impossible and I can't accept it," Hatim shouted in dismay. Lawrence came out of the counter and patted his back. He said, "Son, it's not over yet. You can apply for a reval (re-evaluation) or attempt the supplementary exams in the next few months. After all, you only have three papers to clear." These words didn't console Hatim. Ringing aloud in his head were the monstrous words, "You have failed." Hatim ran out of college and sprinted onto the footpath. Thoughts echoed in his head like a roller coaster, "This is not possible, it's probably a dream. Should I go back and recheck? Could there be a printing mistake? Should I opt for reval? Oh no. I have failed." Hatim ran till he could run no more. He found himself hopping into an empty police booth. Panting for breath, he tried hard to stop the boomeranging thoughts in his head. “This isn’t happening. Was this the curse of my dad? I can’t be in the bottom two. How can I share this with my mom? How can I get back home? What about my career? I have failed.” Hatim tried to stem these thoughts with a loud unintended shout. “Stoppppppppppppp!”

Startled by this loud shout, an auto driver applied the brakes on his autorickshaw and the vehicle came to a screeching halt. Looking up at the police booth, the auto driver was a bit puzzled to see Hatim instead of a policeman. Hatim stepped out and walked towards the auto and asked, “Railway station?” The driver responded with a nod and turned the meter on. Cling.

Chapter 3

THE TRAIN TO NOWHERE

A lot of us would like to move mountains, but few of us are willing to practice on small hills.

- Anonymous

The central tower clock outside the railway station showed 3.55 p.m. Hatim walked into the station empty-handed. All he had with him was rupee currency worth sixty dollars. This was the first time in his life that Hatim had walked into a railway station without knowing where he wanted to go. The man at the ticket counter was a tough looking guy in his mid-forties. He looked sternly at Hatim and asked, "*Kahaan* ('where' in Hindi)?" Hatim replied, "Give me ticket on the first train that will leave the station." It was the Rajdhani Express, a fast train that would take about thirty-hours to Delhi. There couldn't be a better and farther option for Hatim, who wanted to just run away from the entire mess. He asked for a ticket in the sleeper coach, which was luckily available. Hatim walked to the closest phone booth and dialed his home. Five rings later, his mother picked up the phone and said in the usual feeble tone, "*Haan* hello." When she did not get a response, she repeated 'hello' a few times before hanging up. Hatim dialed again. "*Maa,* it's me," said Hatim. His mother asked him where he was and what his exam results were. "I have lost three subjects and I can't believe it. Your son has failed *maa*," he exclaimed. Like any other mother, she told him that these things happened and they didn't really matter in the long run.

She asked him to return home and assured him that his father would be fine with it, if things were explained to him. Hatim was stubborn. He said he was leaving town for some time and he would return when things were better. His mother tried hard to persuade him to stay back. But Hatim was firm. He assured her that he would be fine and that he had to realign his goals and make a comeback.

He made another call to his paying guest accommodation and informed his landlord that he would be out of town for a while. He also informed him that he could rent out his portion to others. He hung up the phone and picked up a bottle of water and a few snacks before boarding the train.

Hatim checked for bogie one and berth number seventy-nine. Was this a coincidence or was this destiny at play, he wondered. Walking into the compartment, he found it empty. He sat down as the train pulled out of the station and gained speed. As he noticed the houses and buildings outside the window disappearing rapidly, he gradually came to terms with his exam results. He sat sipping water with one thought echoing in his mind, "I am treading below zero. What next?"

The train stopped at a station within the city for a quick two-minute halt. Not many people boarded the train. Hatim wondered if he was in the right train. Then he told himself that it didn't matter. He smiled to himself as he took a deep breath and momentary relief set in.

She was tall and athletic with a fair complexion. She was strikingly attractive in a gown. "Is this 76?" she asked in a calm voice, pointing to the berth opposite Hatim. He gathered himself and replied, "Yeah, yes it is." Hatim's thoughts froze with the arrival of an unexpected co-passenger. Not because she was a woman or was attractive. But there was something quite powerful and magnetic about her. She naturally commanded attention.

"Delhi?" she asked and Hatim nodded and said, "Yeah. What about you?" "Gurgaon," she replied. What surprised Hatim was although he had barely spoken two sentences with her, he was able to gather a lot about the woman. He thought she was confident, fearless, independent, modest, elegant, straightforward, calm and peaceful.

"My name is Hatim," he said and extended his right hand forward for a handshake. "I am Naada," she replied with a gentle nod, without extending her hand. Hatim withdrew his hand, a bit uncomfortably.

A few minutes of silence transpired. Naada glanced at her watch and pulled out a prayer mat and spread it on the berth. Excusing herself, she went into a focused and calm meditative state for seven minutes. Hatim could hear only an intermittent murmur. Once she completed her prayer, she greeted Hatim with a nod and pulled out her laptop to work. From the corner of his eyes, Hatim looked at the gadget longingly, as it was not something many owned back then. Naada was working on complicated sheets, graphs and presentations. A few minutes later, Naada closed her laptop and put it back in her bag.

Hatim mustered his guts and asked, "Naada, what do you do in Gurgaon?" Naada replied, "I have a team working in Gurgaon and we are into training, consulting and peak performance coaching."

"Now, what's that?" asked Hatim, clueless about the terminologies.

Naada answered, "We help people in organizations cruise through change due to growth, acquisition or any major reshuffle. We also coach teams and individuals to find and nurture the best within them." Hatim instantly sat up, pleasantly surprised. Curiously he stammered, "Errr... You are a coach and you can help people when they have failed and are extremely confused?"

"Yes, that's one of the areas I work with people and that's what I love to do." Naada had barely completed her sentence, when Hatim almost jumped in his seat and said, "I think God has sent you to help me. This is destiny and I am sure there is a bigger purpose to this meeting."

Baffled, Naada did not know how to respond. The first thought that came to her mind was whether Hatim was trying to flirt with her. Naada was a very strong woman in her mind. She quickly dismissed her assumption about Hatim. "I don't understand what you are saying. Can you be straight please?" she said firmly. Hatim couldn't gather his sentences; he didn't know where to begin. After a few seconds of struggle, he quickly narrated his predicament.

Naada listened very carefully, at times amazed, at times surprised and at times a bit impatient due to Hatim's extensive narration.

When she woke up it was about 5.30 a.m. and the train was zipping past a main junction. Naada realized that she had slept through the last part of Hatim's story. She looked at Hatim who was still asleep in his berth.

Chapter 4

A Window of Hope

Tell a man he is brave, and you help him to become so.

- Thomas Carlyle

Naada slowly pulled out her toothbrush and walked towards the wash area. Returning, she picked up her prayer mat and offered her prayers. It was a beautiful morning with freshness and purity in the air, the kind you seldom experienced in the cities. Naada settled in one of the window seats and began murmuring incantations in a very soft voice.

It was the *chai-wala* who woke up Hatim. It took him a minute to come to reality. A recap of what had transpired, flashed in his mind's eye. With a half-hearted greeting to Naada, he quickly moved away to freshen up. Naada had already bought breakfast and even paid for it. Hatim tried to be formal and polite and asked her why she had paid. Naada did not respond. She opened the breakfast box. She thoughtfully said, "There are three kinds of people in this world: those who make things happen, those who watch things happen and those who wonder what happened. Which group do you belong to?" Hatim was baffled and had no answer. He tried to understand which category he fell under.

Finally, he wondered why he should even think about these categories. He said, "But Naada, why should I categorize myself at all?"

"So, you don't know the answer," Naada responded calmly. "This is the typical answer I get from people who do not know what their purpose in life is and where they are going. This is the thought process of people who deny the need for a direction. People usually deny the truth as it always goes against their comfort. Denying the truth doesn't change the truth. If you don't know who you are, why you are here and where you are going, I am sure you will never find an appropriate road to enjoy a journey worth treading. If you don't have a plan today, you obviously aren't prepared for the challenges of tomorrow. If you do not have a plan for yourself, that is a plan in itself. Also, if you do not have a plan, you will probably become a part of someone else's plan. Many people in this world don't enjoy being a part of someone's plan. Those who don't own goals will have to rent out the goals of others by working for their goals. Even If you have a half-baked plan, it is still a great start. Sincere intentions are solid plans in the making and are usually half the battle won."

Naada paused before continuing, "One thing is for sure, warriors don't shoot in the dark. They have this craving for clarity and thirst for a target. I have worked with many men and women who are very different from ordinary people. They are not always successful and, to a large extent, the results don't matter to them. However, whatever state they are in, they have clarity of who they are, why they are here and where they are heading. Hatim, imagine you have been gifted a BMW. You have a driver's license, good driving skills and a fine highway waiting for you. What are the possible reasons that could stop you from taking the car for a spin?" Hatim was trying to give a logical answer.

Naada continued, "If the windscreen is dirty, would you drive? Or if the signboards are not clear, would you get into the lane? You must switch on the wipers to clean the windscreen. You must ask someone where the highway is before you place your foot on the pedal. If the reasoning is so simple in case of driving a car, why don't we apply this logic to our lives? Having clarity of vision, direction and goals is a very powerful state to be in. Where there is a will, there are always highways. I am willing to help you create some basic certainty in your life, if you are coachable." Hatim was nodding all the way but a question lingered in his mind – what does 'being coachable' mean?"

Chapter 5

ARE YOU COACHABLE?

He who cannot be a good follower, cannot be a good leader.

- Aristotle

"I am sure you want to know what being coachable is, right?" Naada asked. Hatim nodded, wondering how she was able to read his mind.

"Who is the world's best batsman?" Naada asked. Hatim being a passionate cricket follower was quick to answer. "Sachin, of course." Naada nodded and continued, "Do you recall the game in which Sachin miscued a shot at the nightmarish score of ninety-nine and almost got himself out? However, he got through that and scored a century. The entire stadium, the media and the nation cheered and praised him. He then got out to a brilliant delivery at 114 and walked back with his head high, acknowledging the crowd as they give him a standing ovation. The fielders of the opposition clapped for him too. He walked up the stairs of the dressing room where he was greeted by his coach with a flurry of criticism on his wrong stroke at ninety-nine. The harsh lecture went on while the entire world was in praise of Sachin. How do you think Sachin responded?"

Hatim placed himself in Sachin's shoes and said, "Had I been Sachin, I would have been hurt and upset. I probably would have reminded the coach that I was the world's best batsmen and I had made an unconscious error that had to be overlooked. I would have probably escalated the matter to the board."

Naada said, "I cannot imagine Sachin responding in such a manner and this is the quality which makes him coachable. In all probability Sachin would have responded, 'Coach, I get your message. It was a blunder. I was under a bit of pressure and lost my cool. I will work harder to correct this weakness and improve next time.'"

Naada continued, "Sachin is the world's best batsman, not because he has clocked the maximum hours of cricket but because he is coachable. He is a flexible learner. For that, one needs to be a humble listener and an obedient follower. True warriors are coachable even when they are at war. Being coachable is being able to listen to criticism as if it were positive feedback and being grateful for that criticism. It is one of the most superior qualities of people who lead from the front.

"There were many other batsmen who started their careers like Sachin. Some of them were much better in their batting technique and skill. They didn't climb the ladder of success as they were over-confident of their capabilities and not readily coachable. They ceased to learn, became redundant and were eventually dropped from the team. Being coachable is a tough ask as one needs to have or develop the ability to listen to the truth about oneself without a sugar coating.

"While the common reaction to criticism is defense, the one who wishes to stand out must have the ear to receive continuous criticism and still hold on to a state of contemplation and learning. Hatim, are you ready to take this on as a commitment and promise for life? Not only with me while I coach you, but as a principle in life?"

Naada was not done. "We women strongly believe that unless the dough loses its sticky nature, accepts tough kneading and readily becomes soft and moldable, we will never be able to bake the best bread. This seems to be a law of nature and you can see this in all aspects of life."

Hatim took a minute to absorb all that Naada had just said. He asked her to explain the entire rigmarole of being coachable again. She repeated everything with patience. Hatim acknowledged that he hadn't been coachable at all in his life. He said that he was stubborn and believed that whatever he thought and did was right. He believed that being stubborn meant confidence. He said he had ignored what others had said about him all these years.

Naada's explanation shattered the delusion that Hatim had carried all these years. This realization helped him declare to Naada that he was willing to be coached, now and for life. Naada warned him that this would be a tough ask and his identity may need to be consciously rebuilt and that his dear ones would, in all probability, reject him completely. Worst of all, his ego would take a beating. Hatim stood strong and affirmed, "This is the one thing I am clear about – I will be coachable, I will listen, I will learn, I will make things happen. Or else I am heading nowhere. Let us not waste time. Please start and I assure you that you will find me completely coachable and listening with focus." The train moved on.

Chapter 6

Clean Your Slate

When you forgive, you don't change the past, you change the future.

- Anonymous

Naada handed Hatim her huge cell phone, which was a new and rare luxury in the mid-nineties. Hatim was by now getting used to Naada's abrupt ways of throwing questions at him or surprising him. He consciously didn't question her. Instead, he pressed the dial button and looked up at her. He asked, "Number?" Naada replied, "Your home." Hatim was not surprised but he resisted a bit, as he realized that something unpleasant was about to happen.

"Call your dad now and speak to him. You do not need to apologize, just enquire about him and listen." For Hatim, it was a tough call to make. But he had agreed to be coachable and accepted Naada as his coach. Hence, he did not protest. His fingers felt as though they outweighed his hand. One by one, he keyed in the numbers and dialed home. To his relief, an automatic recorded message said that outgoing calls were deactivated from the number. Naada switched off the handset and turned it on again. She redialed Hatim's number and it rang.

Hatim's sister picked up the call and shrieked with joy hearing Hatim's voice. She spoke to him for a while and then handed the phone to her mother. Hatim told her that he was traveling to Delhi to establish something worthwhile and asked her to pray for him. He then surprised his mother with a sudden request, "Mom, can I speak to dad?" Excited she called out aloud to his dad. He came on line and said in his usual curt manner, "*Bolo* (speak)." Hatim was overcome with emotion and couldn't gather the right words.

Hatim mumbled something and then said, "How are you, dad?" The next few minutes, Hatim experienced an unbelievable freedom and lightness. He was able to speak to his father fearlessly. He had assumed that he would choke while talking to the most aggressive man he had ever seen, but he was now leading the conversation. Surprisingly, he found his father responsive. Hatim could even sense uncertainty with a tinge of happiness in his father's voice.

"Dad, I failed in my finals in three subjects but I am confident I will get through in the supplementary tests. I am off to Delhi in pursuit of a few goals, which I am yet to decide. I will come home once I have laid the foundation of what I aspire to do."

For the first time in the conversation, he could hear his father sigh faintly. Hatim was not sure if it was in sorrow, joy or anger. He could visualize his father standing next to the old semi-circular telephone table, withholding his emotions. The tougher people are from outside, the softer they are within. But warriors are just the opposite: they are tougher within and softer outside.

The call went on for twelve minutes but it seemed like an eon. After hanging up, Hatim just couldn't stop smiling as tears of joy rolled down his left cheek and then his right. "Thank you for this," he said, nodding at Naada who was already pulling out a tissue for him. Naada said, "Hatim, now you are good to start. I never paint on a canvas that is already painted. It is always a good practice to clean the mind slate once in a while. Carrying excess baggage, especially when you decide to fly high and far, may not be a wise thing to do. You will end up paying heavily for the excess baggage. The worse reality is that you may get caught up with a few minor goals, which will never allow you to discover the major purpose of your life. Your life and existence are too precious to be taken for granted. If you are not willing to accept and realize this fact, who else can help you do so? Wipe the white board of your life clean, once in a while. And then make this a habit."

When you blame others, you give up your power to change.

- Dr Robert Anthony

"Conflict with your dad was one of the biggest blessings that you probably failed to notice," said Naada.

Hatim was completely puzzled.

"Now let us do an exercise. It is called appreciative thinking. You must objectively appreciate the role of your dad in the conflict. Let us see if you can consciously list the good attributes of your dad and the positive outcomes from his behavior. For this, you have to move out of Hatim's shoes i.e. you need to develop the perspective of a third party to visualize your complete experience with your dad. You will then comment on the entire episode without thinking and emoting like Hatim."

Images of his father's persona flashed in his mind, reminding Hatim of his aggression, stubbornness and non-listening attitude. It was impossible for Hatim to see any goodness in his father or a good outcome that he had caused.

Hatim's face reflected his feelings and Naada was quick to notice. Hatim could not get out of his shoes and get into a third party perspective. Whatever he had experienced with his father over the years was so strong and clear in his mind that he was convinced there could be no other perspective. The phone conversation he had had with his father only helped him overcome his fear and hesitation to communicate with him. It made him feel lighter and free, but there was not even an iota of change in what he felt for his father. The conversation didn't impact his perspective about his father. Forget appreciation, Hatim could not even think of a good deed to attribute to his father.

Hatim looked upset and said, "Naada, you do not understand who my dad is and you are trying to change my feelings towards him. But the reality is I haven't met a meaner person than my father. I may speak to him and listen to what he has to say. I will take care of him as a son, but I cannot change my stance towards him. I cannot find a reason to appreciate him and I will not be able to forget what has transpired over the past. He has been the primary cause of my pain and the misery in my family."

Hatim was in a heightened state of aggression. Naada quickly intervened, "Carl Gustav Jung, the scientist who founded analytical psychology, stated, 'Everything that irritates us about others can lead us to an understanding of ourselves.'"

Naada gave Hatim a glass of water and they took a break. She allowed him to settle down for a while. Both of them stared out of the window. The sun was descending. The fields passing by communicated the vast expanse of goodness, prosperity, growth, life and possibilities to Naada. It had no meaning to Hatim as he was still pulling himself out of his past. He kept telling himself, "I must be coachable. I must listen and obey." Finally, an hour later, he said, "I am fine and ready to be coached."

Chapter 7

Coconuts or Nothing

"We human beings are the products of our communication, convictions, beliefs, values and habits, not necessarily in that order. Look at this," said Naada and drew an image on a sheet of paper.

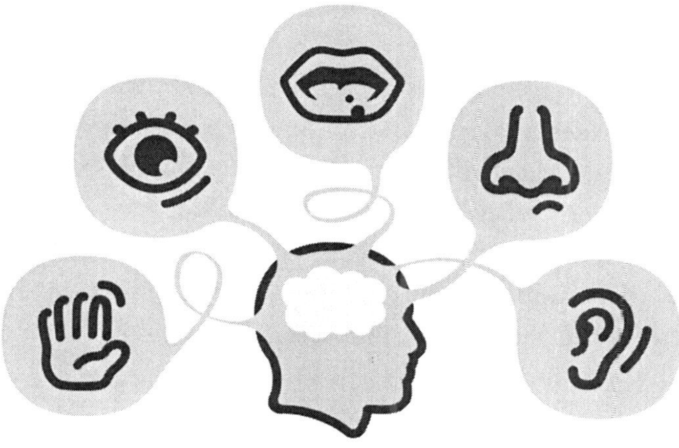

"We have five dynamic senses that help us perceive the world i.e. seeing, hearing, feeling, tasting and smelling, as represented in the picture. However, three senses represent our major capabilities and predominantly influence our experience of the world. They are seeing, hearing and feeling, also termed **visual** (anything we see externally or imagine internally), **auditory** (anything we hear externally or listen internally) and **kinesthetic** (anything we feel and do physically and feel internally; this includes the experience of taste and smell), respectively. These three channels are the gateway to any knowledge and wisdom we acquire. We usually use the common term 'our world' but in reality we understand and relate to only 'my world' as these are my senses and they are unique to me. Any event I perceive is unique and different from what you perceive. This is the reason we get so many views about the same accident, incident, wedding, business or a person."

Naada continued sketching a detailed picture. Hatim watched amazed. Naada spoke as she sketched, "Relating to life is not an easy process but it becomes easy if we acknowledge the supreme design of the human mind and what makes it operate effectively. Driving a Formula 1 car could be a big challenge unless we have enough knowledge about it or we have been instructed on how it works, right? Our mind is more powerful and complex than any machine ever built. Understanding how it works can help us make life easier, effective and more in control."

Hatim was convinced with what Naada had said and was ready to grasp and absorb every bit of information she was about to share.

Naada consciously avoided talking about Hatim's father. She went on to share a few interesting facts which Hatim agreed to. He said 'yes' or nodded in agreement, now and then. Naada watched his body language and observed his tone. Once she was convinced that he was really ready and listening, she continued.

Habits are cobwebs at first; cables at last.

- A Chinese proverb

"An egg can be broken in two ways – either from the outside or from the inside. When broken from outside, a life ends; when broken from inside, a life begins. Any change, transformation or turnaround predominantly happens inside out, not outside in. Most of us work on our habits and behavior to achieve changes. This is just a reflection of who we are on the outside. We do get results but they are just obtainable and not sustainable.

"Hatim, have you seen the elephant in the circus performing acts that amaze us? How can a beast so mighty and strong be trained to behave in such a timid and disciplined way? The primary job of a mahout (elephant trainer) in the circus is to tame wild elephant calves. He cannot get results by beating up the animals. The elephant calves can get wilder and more aggressive than what they already are. The first intent for the mahout is to get the little elephant to accept that it is now a part of the circus and cannot escape from it. This is a process that needs to be conditioned internally for the elephant. So the mahout ties down the elephant with a very strong iron chain. Over the next few days, the elephant tries to break free many times but fails.

"Gradually, the external experiences help form a strong internal opinion, which further translates into a gut feeling for the elephant in its own language. The elephant soon accepts that whatever it does, it cannot escape. Thus, it stops trying to escape. A couple of days later, you will see the little elephant comfortably sitting down and enjoying whatever is provided as food. A few days more and the elephant feels at home and the acceptance that 'this is my home and I live here' strengthens in the animal. The mahout has won the battle. He now unlocks the iron chain and replaces it with an insignificant rope nailed to a tiny peg on the ground. No matter what, the elephant will stay put wherever the mahout decides to keep him. With the newly conditioned feeling, the elephant is ready to get trained to perform at the circus. This is the same case with human beings. We are creatures who operate on the fuel of many such gut feelings."

Naada sketched a coconut tree as Hatim watched with curiosity. She asked Hatim, "Have you seen a coconut tree in the coastal region?"

Hatim nodded in the affirmative.

Naada continued, "When there are strong winds along the coast, what happens to these coconut trees?" Hatim said, "They sway in the direction of the wind." "Exactly!" exclaimed Naada. "The trees change position and move but the minute the wind stops, the trees return to their original positions. We humans are just like these trees. The moment we get motivated, read a success story or hear an inspiring talk, we decide to change and start working on our habits and behavior. We do experience change but, as I said earlier, this change is momentary, similar to the change the coconut tree experienced. It has novelty value. The moment the wind of motivation stops, we are back to our original old habits and behavior."

Naada continued sketching even as she spoke. "The trunk of the tree represents the habits and behavior on which the winds act but what holds this massive trunk in position are the strong roots, which are unseen. Our habits and behavior are like the trunk of the tree, which is visible. We tend to focus on our habits and behavior to achieve change. What is unseen within us and comparable to the roots of the tree is the gut feeling we have. These gut feelings are our convictions and beliefs that govern and control us.

Belief system - The Master Key to Sustainable Transformation

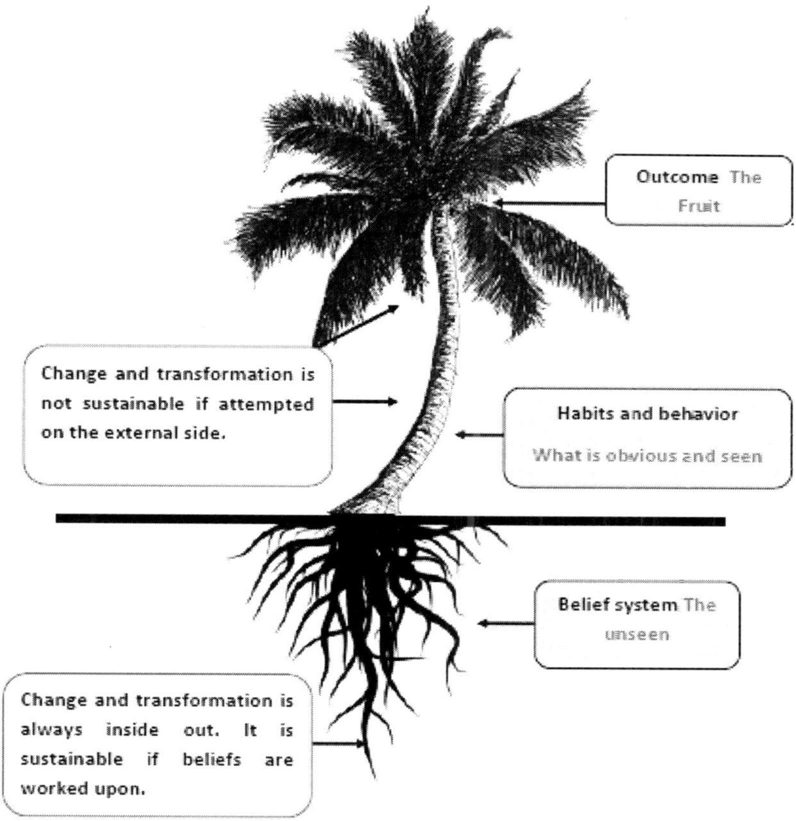

"Like the elephant's beliefs, our beliefs are also formed and strengthened over a period of time through an amazing process of repetitive learning, constant modeling and rigorous conditioning. We cannot have sustainable change and transformation in our habits and behavior unless we work with intensity to identify and transform our existing limiting beliefs.

"The coconut tree cannot have a sustainable change unless it is uprooted and moved to another supportive environment. The process of uprooting is tougher than planting a tree. There is conscious and careful hard work required. However, if the primary intent of the individual is to experience transformation, the process becomes relatively easier and quicker."

Hatim felt something strange happening to him. He was already able to see many possibilities through the metaphor of the coconut tree.

Naada continued, "We are not taught to understand how a belief takes birth and builds within us. Our education system does not have any structured method of revealing it to us. Hence, most of us unconsciously and blindly adapt to the readily available system of beliefs from our immediate social mirrors – our parents, relatives, friends, peers and society. We struggle with our habits and behavior, not because we don't want to change, but because we do not understand the root cause that drives our behavior. We don't know how to achieve a sustainable change.

"We get angry for the same specific reasons and regret after the damage is done. We fear the same causes and live in this state whenever confronted with them. We get frustrated with the same tasks and feel helpless doing them. We eat what is damaging to our health and end up feeling guilty about it. The list goes on. The primary reason we accept our bad habits and give up on changing them is because we have nurtured them perfectly by chance but we do not have a clue how to change them by choice. This is where hopelessness sets in and it is certainly not a good place to be in.

"Let us move ahead to a solution-oriented approach. Let us decipher the hidden codes of our mental program that will help us run a quality check and identify the bugs. The next logical step is to make the necessary shifts to resolve the bugs and build a more powerful code to achieve our own scale and meaning of success."

With renewed vigor, Naada continued, "Generalization, distortion and deletion (GDD) are special capacities of our brain to filter, test, validate, pick, choose, and ignore information and experiences to help us shape our mental makeup, in short the software of our minds. Generalization is taking something specific and applying it to a broad context. It's a generalization to say all cats chase squirrels. Distortion is a change, twist or exaggeration that makes something appear different from what it really is. You can distort a visual image, a thought or even an idea. To say you don't keep yourself spic and span is a distortion of facts as it is highly debatable what 'spic and span' means. One more example is when you call someone 'cool.' 'Cool' is again not definable. Deletion is a process by which a visual, a thought, sounds or information is left out. To get accustomed to the noise of a rickety ceiling fan after a while is deletion of the sound. To focus on one aspect of the scene and miss out or ignore the other details is deletion of some of the visuals of that scene.

"GDD has a direct influence on what is seen, heard, felt and represented internally. In short, you have a thought, visual, sound or feeling that can be generalized, distorted or deleted. Hatim, I want you to focus and understand this aspect of our mind. Once you understand and accept this fact, it will be easier for you to deal with your own emotions and, more importantly, the reactions of others. I will explain this to the best of my ability and pray that you get the essence of the message.

"Focus on the image I have sketched below. It explains the entire cycle of how our mind processes information and experiences. Anything that happens around us is experience; it has the elements of visuals, sounds and feelings captured by our senses and processed by our brain through the conscious and/or subconscious mind. This information, on repetitive filtering and conditioning, creates our belief system. Our belief system makes us who we are and obviously reflects in our actions, behavior and habits.

"Filtering is a choice. Hence, we must develop a filtering process that helps us validate and create empowering beliefs that complement our primary purpose in life. Our belief system, though fluid, is an internal gut feeling and a sense of certainty that controls our external behavior. We have both positive empowering beliefs and negative disempowering beliefs. If you don't work to choose a productive belief system, you will end up with a set of random beliefs that will choose you.

"More often than not, randomly chosen beliefs can be detrimental to our purpose in life. They can make us lose our power of choice, breed weakness in our decision-making and create a whole load of confusion in the structure of thoughts that navigate our brain cells. People with a weak belief system are usually uncertain about their purpose, direction and decision. They make wrong choices and end up blaming others or complaining about the unfavorable outcomes of the wrong choices made."

Chapter 8

TERMITES OR TREASURES – BOTH ARE HIDDEN

Naada was intense now and began. "Before we consciously build a set of powerful and positive beliefs, we must understand how to identify the beliefs already stored within us. Beliefs are hidden subconsciously and they reflect the character of our inner being. The fact is we are who we are inside. We may be housing beliefs with a similitude of termites that work hard and relentlessly to destroy us from within or we may have a store of hidden treasures waiting to be discovered and utilized. Working to minimize or eradicate termites is our primary goal. Wisdom suggests that we must first work on dealing with the termites and then embark on the treasure hunt.

"So let us get hold of a few simple yet profound proven ways that can help us clean up the bugs completely. These methods have been used by the league of extraordinary human beings, either naturally on their own or through a learning process. Modeling these concepts will help us achieve the same results. Hatim, you need to give hundred percent of your focus now. If you have any questions, do not hesitate to stop me and clarify. This will help you grasp, chew and digest the concepts better.

"We all have a set of defined beliefs in the following six major areas of our life. These areas are common to everyone, but the beliefs vary."

Naada used the writing pad again and wrote these.

The important areas of our life with an example each:

- About **ME (Identity)** – E.g., I am an extrovert and I can speak to strangers.
- About **MY FAMILY (Relationships)** – E.g., My dad doesn't understand me.
- About **OTHERS (Society)** – E.g., I have received from others, I must give back.
- About **WEALTH (Assets)** – E.g., I don't plan my wealth, hence I can't save.
- About **HEALTH (Fitness)** – E.g., I can't give up sweets, hence I am overweight.
- About **PURPOSE (Spirituality)** – E.g., God helps those who help themselves.

"Hatim, these are a few probable empowering and disempowering beliefs I have coined as examples. Our behavior, habits and action are in alignment with the individual beliefs I have coined. I am sure you can guess what behavior or action I would take in case I carry each one of these beliefs."

Naada went on sketching images and boxes as Hatim watched in awe.

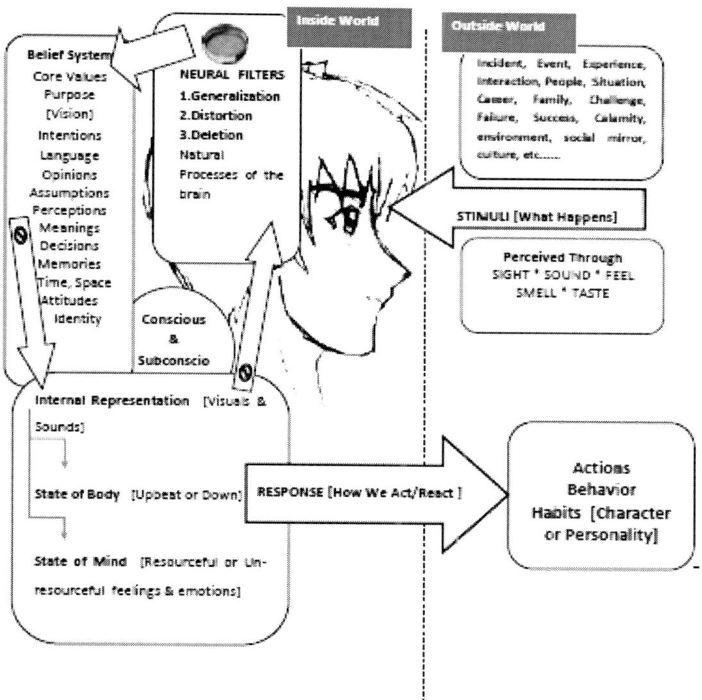
Inside World
Outside World
Belief System
Core Values
Purpose
[Vision]
Intentions
Language
Opinions
Assumptions
Perceptions
Meanings
Decisions
Memories
Time, Space
Attitudes
Identity
NEURAL FILTERS
1.Generalization
2.Distortion
3.Deletion
Natural Processes of the brain
Conscious & Subconscio
Incident, Event, Experience, Interaction, People, Situation, Career, Family, Challenge, Failure, Success, Calamity, environment, social mirror, culture, etc......
STIMULI [What Happens]
Perceived Through
SIGHT * SOUND * FEEL
SMELL * TASTE
Internal Representation [Visuals & Sounds]
State of Body [Upbeat or Down]
State of Mind [Resourceful or Un-resourceful feelings & emotions]
RESPONSE [How We Act/React]
Actions
Behavior
Habits [Character or Personality]

Chapter 9

PIZZA

PIZZA DELIGHT

"Hatim, imagine you have an **intention** to have a good dinner out with your family. A friend had suggested one of the finest pizza joints in town, a tiny outlet called PizzaPark. You take your family there and you all have an extraordinary experience. You have a **Significant Emotional Experience** recorded through your senses of sight, sound, smell, taste and feeling processed by your conscious mind and stored in your memory.

"You reaffirm your **opinion** of this outlet by seeing, hearing and feeling what the other members of your family have to express. They claim to have had a similar, if not the same, experience as you have. You visit this outlet again and have the same experience. You again reaffirm your opinion, which now grows to become a **belief.** Your mind associates this experience as an **internal representation** of visuals, sounds, taste, smell and feelings that trigger a positive upbeat **physical state,** an emotion of joy and a delightful **state of mind.** Hence, your natural **response** to any discussion on pizza would be a recommendation of this tiny PizzaPark outlet as though you were paid for every pizza sold here. Your visualization, memory, internal dialogue and opinion about PizzaPark is nothing but an experience of delight.

"So every time you think of PizzaPark, your **internal representation** triggers an upbeat **body** and a resourceful

mind. I call it the Green Strategy. More so, when you wish to have pizza, your **reaction** invariably is to opt for this outlet due to the **belief of excellence** you associate with this outlet. Many people having a similar opinion can create a **generalized** statement in the circle. PizzaPark pizzas are the best in the town becomes an accepted **belief** among a large group of people."

The flow chart below shows the formation of a belief.

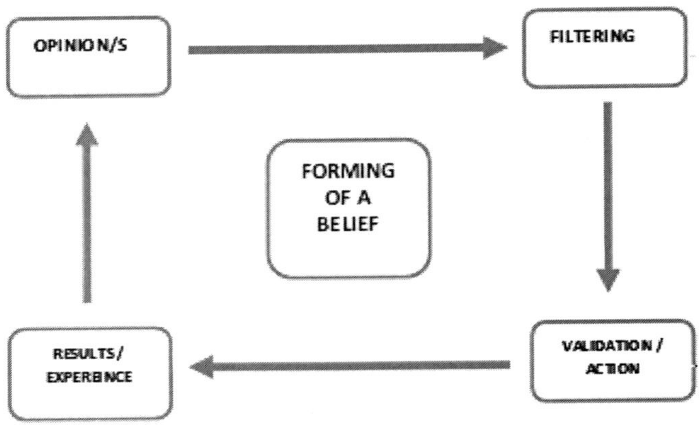

Forming of a BELIEF – The tabletop is the belief and the legs are the opinions.

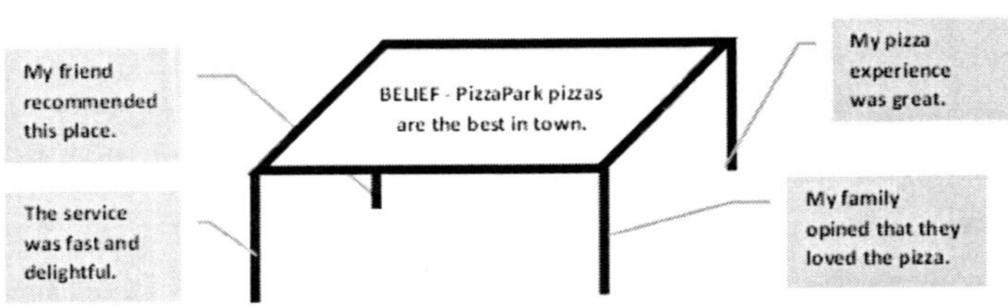

SEE – Significant Emotional Experience – Green Strategy

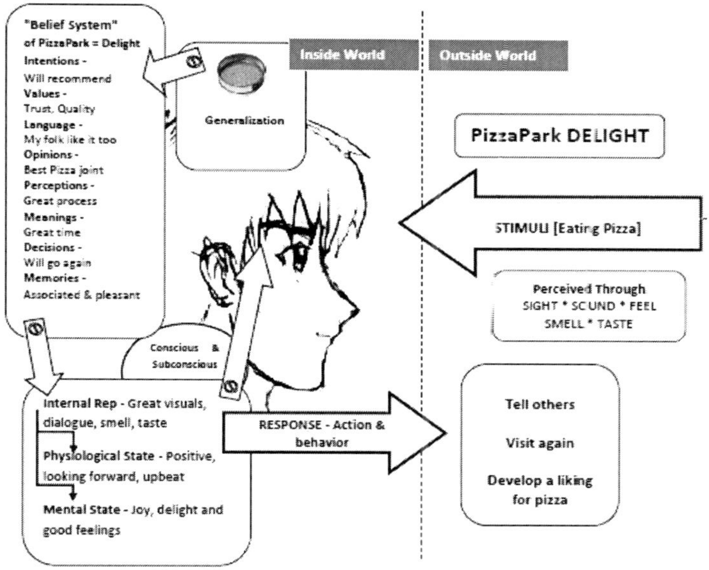

PIZZA DISASTER

"It is your twelfth visit to your favorite pizza outlet. While having the penultimate bite of the last pizza slice, you discover the legs of a cockroach in it. You let out a glass-shattering shriek. This is obviously an unbelievable shock. This is a **Significant Emotional Experience** as well. The probable filter in operation now is **distortion or deletion** as the information you have at hand is incomplete. You probably experience a major internal conflict with your existing **belief** about PizzaPark.

"Your own statement and internal representation about PizzaPark is now at stake and your mind is unable to handle this. Values such as trust, honesty, integrity and quality are in question. Hatim, please keep referring to the images as I speak. Your mind is under severe stress and confusion. The disaster continues. You summon the manager who starts off with an apology but when you express more of your disappointment, he gets defensive and says that such things do happen and you should not make it a big issue. Your values, assumptions, memory, representation and visualization do not allow you to accept this experience. You have now **distorted** and incomplete information with you. So you take go inside to inspect the kitchen. A bigger shock awaits you there.

"Your mind is now flooded with leg-breaker opinions and questions. You find it to be one of the most horrible kitchens you have ever seen: pathetic infrastructure, badly maintained utensils, roaches all around, cobwebs on the windows, chef in a dirty state and unkempt cooks with dirty hands and dark dirty nails. Your earlier **belief** about this outlet comes crashing and a new **belief** replaces it. You now go out and tell the same people your new opinion and the new reality that has dawned you. If you have enough proof, the **generalized** belief about PizzaPark could change for others as well."

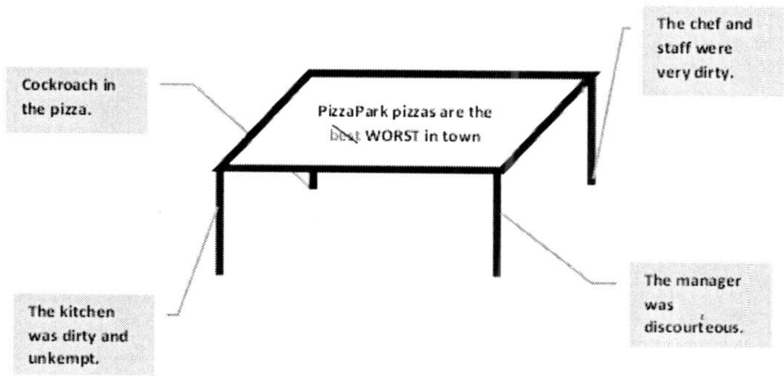

Collapse of a BELIEF by a LEG-BREAK – New belief [tabletop] & new opinions [legs]

SEE (Significant Emotional Experience) – Red Strategy

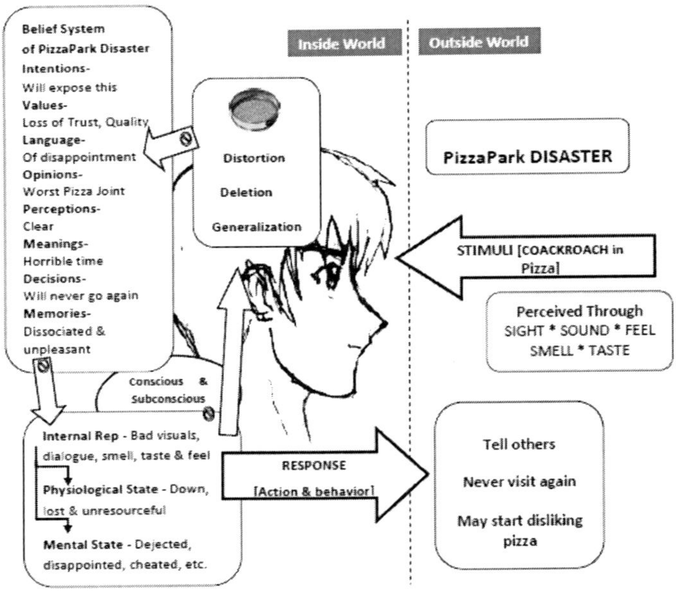

Hatim understood the concept of generalization and distortion but was a bit puzzled about deletion. He asked Naada to explain it again. He also wanted to know the connection with his father's attributes and behavioral outcomes. Naada continued, "Hatim, don't worry about its connection with your dad. We can talk about it later. I first wish to explain a bit more about the **deletion** capability of our mind. Are you with me?" Hatim nodded in the affirmative as his focus about his father faded away. He was ready to listen to what Naada was about to share.

"**Deletion** is the capability of the brain to ignore anything we don't like, aren't comfortable with and don't want to deal with. It is another capacity of the brain to ignore information completely. Our mental filters are filled and clogged with assumptions and perceptions that are usually generalized, distorted or deleted. Deletion helps us naturally exempt information that may be of low importance or relevance to us. This is the reason when you walk into a fish market, the initial smell is unbearable. But after you spend a few minutes there, you are no more sensitive to the smell. The brain deletes the smell though the smell is as strong as it was when you walked in. The smell hasn't changed but your brain chooses to ignore it. The same happens in a perfume shop or with this rickety train window. You have been sitting here for almost two days. You may have noticed its irritating rattling sound for the first few minutes when the train moved. But later, your thoughts and focus allowed you to delete this unpleasant noise completely from your mind." Hatim nodded his head vigorously as he understood the example of the noisy window. "This capability of the brain can be used for better purposes consciously and to develop the habit of **selective deletion**," said Naada.

Hatim was amazed at the information Naada had. Where on earth did this girl get such profound knowledge, he wondered. His thoughts were interrupted by Naada's voice. "Let us go back to the same PizzaPark example. Let us assume it is now over three years since the cockroach incident and you have moved out of the city. Your mind gradually deletes most elements related to the episode as you have moved on. You do not attach much importance to what had occurred in the past. The intensity of your unpleasant emotions is almost zilch.

"GDD explains the simple processes in our brain. These capacities have been bestowed on us to filter, test and validate information and experiences that enable us to shape our mental makeup or inner being. The primary reason why we have these capabilities is to achieve our Truly Important Goals [TIG] in life. More importantly, GDD helps us avoid getting caught in petty and insignificant issues.

"If our mental filters operate randomly, without being trained and aligned to our purpose, they will eventually get clogged with perceptions and assumptions without apt verification and reasoning. Legends and extraordinary individuals learn to simplify these abilities and use them to enhance their internal representation, emotional state and physiology. Hence, they maintain a resourceful state most of their life. This is the reason you see a few people who are always cheerful, happy and action-oriented despite having ship loads of challenges and adversities, constantly trying to sink them. They are like warriors and invariably achieve the maximum outcomes while at war.

"As long as the filtering process of GDD helps us achieve our goals in all areas of life, we must learn to adapt and train ourselves to utilize this capability to its best. However, in the journey of seeking excellence one must be very careful and conscious about these filters. One wrong generalization can cause havoc at times. For e.g., there is a popular perception that all daughters-in-law rob the sons from their mothers. This statement has generalization and distortion in it. If a would-be mother-in-law accepted this opinion, it would create an 'already always' internal representation (internal visual or assumptive image) of a would-be daughter-in-law in accordance to the statement. Though the son is still far from choosing a life partner, the way his mother deals with prospective marriage proposals will be influenced by this belief. Her behavior and action towards her daughter-in-law, when she gets one, will be tailored to the belief she has nurtured. I am sure you can imagine the outcome of the relationship between the mother and her daughter-in-law. Then there is the GDD opinion that mothers-in-law are monsters."

Hatim chuckled, "No wonder I see most of my relatives in a mess due to these popular limiting beliefs."

Naada beamed as Hatim was able to grasp these concepts with ease. She was a strong believer in unconditional mentoring when she came across someone hungry for knowledge and committed for change.

She continued, "A common generalized and distorted belief in India is that you cannot get any government related work done if you do not pay a bribe. This generalization is accepted by everyone as an absolute. Hence, no one resists it or attempts otherwise. As a matter of fact, people openly add this cost to products and services. It is unfortunately embedded in our culture and has percolated strongly into the corporate world too. To win contracts, vendors are compelled to pay kickbacks. Many professionals have disclosed that they had to grease the hands of the department head to get a good job offer. To get a professional seat in a college, donations are collected in the name of 'building funds.' This is an outcome of the public having accepted this practice of transaction without resisting it. The public usually accepts any opinion as long as it adds comfort and ease to their way of life. Hence, ethics and principles are put aside as 'ideal gyan' and not a practical concept to implement.

"However, an extraordinary few in this world do not accept any opinion, news, rumor or information unless they have scrutinized and validated it. They do not go by generalized views and distorted information. They stand up against the tide and question the issue. These are the ones who face heavy resistance and confrontation. Their actions and behavior are quite significantly different. They would probably put in extra efforts to look for processes that will get the job done without paying a bribe or a kickback. These people don't survive as one among the crowd but they wish to stand out and lead from the front. They understand their purpose in life clearly.

"Hatim, let us invest some efforts to learn how this league of a few extraordinary people stand out and achieve the impossible and armor themselves against the popular unethical beliefs that the masses succumb to. Let us explore how we can implement small and seemingly insignificant changes in our mental filters and internal representations to experience the warrior within."

Chapter 10

Bulletproof Your Mind

How you see the world depends on the color of the glasses you wear on your mind.

- Anonymous

"Hatim, in life you are bound to be bombarded with experiences, situations and people who can trigger or create generalizations, distortions and deletions every day. How can you identify them? How can you handle them to keep your **internal representation,** followed by your **physical state and mental state,** in a peak resourceful form most of the time? How would you bulletproof your mind? Go slow with me on this as it takes time to get familiar with this subject, but it carries profound significance in self-development sciences. Hatim, you first need to relate to and understand the statement I have penned down here."

90% OF INFORMATION TRANSMITTED TO THE BRAIN IS VISUAL, AND VISUALS ARE PROCESSED 60,000X FASTER IN THE BRAIN THAN TEXT.

Naada continued, "Having said this, we have both visual and textual processes at play in tandem to build the human memory and mental makeup. If you have allowed a random process to take charge of how you internally represent experiences, the ninety percent probability is that you will end up with all the negative brain baggage. You will be in an unresourceful state with the mind more inclined to predominantly unpleasant emotions that ordinary people exhibit. This is because we are creatures who copy, emulate and model. We mirror our immediate environment, follow social norms and adapt to popular rituals. I wish to share with you a few simple yet very effective tools that will help you understand what is going on inside your wiring up there (Naada pointed to Hatim's head) and effectively retain what helps you in your grand purpose of life and do away with what is unnecessary."

"Hatim, don't imagine a pink donkey," said Naada. Hatim was a bit puzzled. Naada continued, "So what happened inside your head?" Hatim disclosed, "I did imagine a pink donkey." Naada asked, "So did you see the text 'pink donkey' or the picture of a pink donkey in your mind?" Hatim said, "Of course, the picture." Naada asked, "Have you ever seen a pink donkey before?" Hatim said smiling, "Nope." Naada continued, "So do you understand the speed and format in which our brain processes information? Also do u understand that the brain does not take a negative command? If you ever tell a kid not to do something, he or she ends up doing it immediately. Our brains do not have the capability to imagine the 'not doing' part. So in the command 'don't imagine a pink donkey' the word 'don't' is deleted or ignored as it is not relatable. Even before I ended my question, the image of a pink donkey appeared on your mind's screen, right?"

Hatim was all smiles, as though he had made a path-breaking discovery. He exclaimed, "Wow, I never realized this fact of my amazing capabilities." Naada seemed to ignore this statement and continued, "Your internal representation and state (physiological and mental) is a result of this strong visualization process and the vocabulary you carry within." Hatim nodded his head, but displayed a big question mark on his face. Naada reassured him, "This seems a bit confusing, but don't worry, I will try to simplify the matter." She moved on, "Hatim, close your eyes, take a deep breath and concentrate on your breathing. Inhale, exhale and relax your body completely." She kept repeating this a few times until Hatim seemed relaxed and calm, amidst the intermittent noise of the railway track and, of course, the rickety window.

"Now imagine and visualize a beautiful and colorful garden. You are taking a walk in this garden barefoot. The grass is soft and moist; you feel the softness of the grass as you walk. There is a gentle and cool breeze touching your face. You see the beautiful flowers, birds and trees. You see the various shapes, sizes and colours of nature around you.

"Listen to the pleasant sounds around. Notice the sounds you may have ignored. As you walk further, you see your house at the beginning of one of the pathways. You walk towards your house and open the gates. You gently knock on the door and your mother opens it and welcomes you the way she always does. You give her a hug. Experience your emotions at this moment (Naada pauses). You follow her into the kitchen. She picks up your favourite pickle and offers you a bite. You enjoy the experience and relish the pickle (she pauses again). You pick up the remote and switch on the TV and find your favourite show playing. You play with the volume control, the colours and the contrast. You watch the program go from color to black and white, from soft to loud and so on. You tune the picture and volume to suit your needs and enjoy the program for the next few seconds (Naada pauses). Observe how engaged you are with the show you like. Then you switch channels and find the program you hate the most playing. You watch this program attentively for a few seconds (Naada pauses). You reduce the volume, make the picture black and white. Observe how the program experience shifts from unpleasant to tolerable.

"You then hear a knock on the door. You walk to the door to open it and see your father at the door. You respond the way you do usually. Experience your emotions at this moment (pause). You wish to leave home now. So you say goodbye to your parents and walk out of the main door back to the garden. As you walk on the grass, you step on a sharp thorn. You feel pain and discomfort (pause). You remove the thorn and continue walking until you find a very big tree. You sit under the shade and lie down to relax (pause). You experience the pleasant shade and the ideal breeze. You then take a deep breath and enjoy a state of relaxation. You inhale, exhale and relax your body completely (pause). On the count of five, you slowly open your eyes."

Once this exercise was done, Naada asked Hatim, "What was your experience?" Hatim had never done anything like this before and had thoroughly enjoyed this exercise. He said, "It was like a dream, an almost real one. It seemed very real."

Naada said, "You imagined the people and situations I narrated and emoted accordingly. All the visuals were played live in your mind, all the sounds were audible and the feeling was real, right? The response to these visuals, sounds and feeling was as real as reality. You were emotional while imagining meeting your mother, you relished the pickle and salivated and you would have had mixed emotions while meeting your dad, right?" Hatim replied, "Absolutely." "This happens to us because the brain does not differentiate between a real experience and a vivid imagination," said Naada.

"Hatim, all these years you have invested your efforts in storing random memories in the form of visuals, sounds and feelings. You associated a preferred convenient meaning to each of them. The total package of what is available in the space of your memory and the beliefs you carry is who you are currently. You will have to work hard to make changes in many of the unwanted beliefs you carry and turn them around to favorable beliefs that will help you achieve something noble and significant in life." This exercise was slowly creating a major shift within Hatim and he felt his soul lighten and body surprisingly energized.

Naada noticed the evident shift but continued, "There are three simple steps I have used in transformational vocabulary that will gradually help you resolve your disempowering memories, negative visuals and unfavourable emotions into empowering ones."

STEP 1

Naada who was now sitting upright, with both her hands held high, began, "Mom and I were at the dinner table when she asked me to bring honey from the kitchen cupboard. As I walked up to the cupboard, which was a good 15 feet away, I had this thought repeatedly running in my mind – *I will not be able to find the honey bottle.*

"As I reached the cupboard, I called out, 'Mom, where is the honey?' My mom replied, 'In the tall glass bottle with a yellow lid, on the left corner of the second shelf.' As I was listening to her, the same old sentence was repeatedly running in my mind – *I will not be able to find the honey bottle.* So, I wasn't able to find the bottle. I called out to my mom again and this went on, back and forth, for a few times. Finally, my mom was tired of instructing me. She walked up to the cupboard and with an exclamation pointed out, 'What is this?'

"The honey bottle was right in front as though staring at me. I was appalled and apologetic. Hatim, if you notice, I repeatedly used the same sentence *I will not be able to find the honey bottle.* This sentence triggered a blind spot in my brain, which further made me believe that the bottle was not there, though it was right in front of me. I am sure we all have had similar experiences."

Hatim responded, "Now I understand why I was unable to find my socks in the wash on most occasions, while my mom would get them in an instant, right in front of me. I would start the sock hunt with the thought that the socks may not be in the wash running in my head, while I rummaged through all the ruffled clothes. This example may seem silly and insignificant, but it certainly is a reality check for me. It is amazing that for all these years I never realized that, in the larger context of life, the language inside my head was dictating my state of mind and beliefs. Changing my inner vocabulary is the window to transforming my outer world. I have lived all these years with an internal conversation of hopelessness and defeat. My internal talk has not been of great quality. Oh God, I have wasted so many productive years in useless self-defeating conversations. I want to make amends. Yes, I want to make appropriate changes and I want to make them starting now. I can't afford to lose any more time living an ordinary life. If it is destiny that I have met you, I do not want to waste what remains of my life over petty stuff."

Naada allowed him to reaffirm his convictions, as these were moments that would allow significant shifts in Hatim's mental landscape. As she watched him, she made short notes of the observations she was able to capture. Hatim was in a peak motivated state and making significant decisions as he spoke. Naada wished to correct him on a few aspects but stopped herself as her wisdom cautioned her intellect. After allowing Hatim to express himself completely, she began, "Incantation means to repeat a word, phrase or sentence. We have in our vocabulary many oft-repeated words and unconsciously favourite patterns of usage. We all have favourite key words that pop up all the time. People around us identify us with these words and phrases, though we may be unaware of using them often.

"Incantations are powerful as they reinforce opinions and help form visuals, sounds and feelings that can gradually build beliefs. What you say often is what you will believe in; the vice-versa is true as well. Many common metaphors are used as incantations. Probably that's why all faiths in this world recommend some daily incantations. You will find spiritual leaders murmuring a few powerful phrases in a disciplined schedule or whenever possible."

Hatim interjected, "Yes, I see you do this often after your prayers and meditation, right?"

Naada smiled and replied, "Yes, I do. We all need constant incantations to reinforce our inner conversations and our beliefs and get rid of our negative beliefs. We are bombarded with loads of negative and de-motivating information every day. About ninety-five percent of the thoughts we nurture every day are negativities carried forward from the previous day. Easy access to news and events leads to an overload of information that is detrimental to our emotional being. Hatim, explore your vocabulary and identify the negative incantations, replace them with positive chants. Search for good self-motivating incantations and make them a habit. A good old friend of mine, whenever asked how he was, never uttered the clichés 'fine' or 'good' but always responded with surprising statements such as, 'If I were any better, I would be twins.' Indeed, he lived as though he had the enthusiasm and energy of two people. Words and sentences that we repeat often have a very profound impact on us and hence they are worth all the attention you can give."

STEP 2

Naada said, "Sweet." And again she stressed the word 'sweeeet.' Then she paused while Hatim looked without a blink. She continued, "We live in a society that is familiar with pain, frustration, failure and lots more. If you tell anyone that you are happy, it will raise many eyebrows. People may wonder if you are normal or you need a visit to the shrink. They will talk behind you. We are so used to listening to exaggerated negative emotions that we fall prey to them. A minor headache is described as 'explosive', a normal hungry feeling is announced as 'famished', a child who is a slow learner is labelled a 'double dodo dumb.' Any such phrase creates visuals that act as pillars to our beliefs. What you say with intensity is what you will experience. Note the high intensity of expression in these phrases."

Hatim interrupted, "Naada, this one is easy and completely relatable. I have been at the receiving end of many such statements."

Naada continued, "Hatim, always reduce the intensity of negative phrases and increase the intensity of positive phrases. We can reframe the above phrases with these: *I have a slight discomfort in my head, I could do with some snacks, the child is a thinker.* Do you get it?" Hatim nodded affirmatively.

"Also, I observed your affirmations a while ago when we were talking about incantations. I picked a word you use often – want. Let me quote you. You said, 'I **want** to make repairs. Yes, I **want** to make appropriate changes and I **want** to make them starting now. I can't afford to lose any more time living an ordinary life. If it is destiny that I have met you, I do not **want** to waste what remains of my life over petty stuff.'

"Transformational vocabulary helps us change such unconscious words to more positive and intense words such as 'must.' Let us see the impact of rephrasing your sentences."

Naada wrote the sentences on another sheet of paper and Hatim read them aloud, "I **must** make repairs. Yes, I **must** make appropriate changes and I **must** make them starting now. I **must** not afford to lose any more time living an ordinary life. If it is destiny that I have met you, I **must** not waste what remains of my life over petty stuff."

Hatim beamed as he said, "The word '**want**' made my desire seem like a soft wish; my affirmation had an element of doubt tagging along. But the moment I said the word 'must', there was a feeling of certainty, commitment and control. This seems so insignificant but it is really so powerful. This is just awesome Naada, and I am getting the hang of transformational vocabulary. I am sure you have more tips up your sleeves."

STEP 3

"If I have to disclose one master key that helps us form or collapse visuals and beliefs, it is this."

Naada surprised Hatim with a rapid fire round. "Eight plus three," she said. And Hatim in an instant responded, "Eleven."

Naada continued, "Capital of Thailand." Hatim said, "Bangkok."

"Number of bones in the human body."

Hatim shot back, "206."

Both smiled. Hatim had the smile of a confused kid and Naada had the smile of a victorious quiz master. Hatim asked, "What was that?" Naada said, "Why did you answer when they were not questions? I never asked you for an answer." Hatim said, "I assumed that I had to answer." Naada said, "Hatim, the operating system that runs our brain predominantly treats information as questions. The responses to any known and unknown information is treated as an enquiry. Any internal conversation is in a question-and-answer format. Hence, our brain fires back responses unconsciously and instantly. The crux to transformation is the format of questions we ask ourselves. The quality of our life is a reflection of the quality of questions we ask ourselves.

"Let me give you an example. Obesity is a huge problem across the globe and the health and wellness industry churns billions of dollars from this. However, the problem seems to get bigger and more serious. Have you wondered why?" Hatim gestured in the negative.

Naada said, "Because people continue to ask the wrong questions to themselves. This leads them to visualize themselves as obese and they continue to believe that they have a problem. Most people ask the wrong questions with high intensity and repeated incantations – *Why am I so fat?* The brain is bound to respond instantly with a flurry of natural answers. *You are irresponsible, you are not disciplined, you overeat, you can't keep up your word, you have no time, exercising is painful, you don't love yourself, you are a loser,* and so on.

"Hatim, all we need to do is turn unresourceful questions into resourceful ones. How about asking – *how can I lose weight?* The same brain offers possibilities like such as: *start a short exercising schedule at home, establish this habit for three months and then join a gym, diet on weekdays, play a game you played in your younger days, cut down on sweets, reach out to alternative therapies, have a moderate lifestyle, avoid parties,* and so on.

"**Questions** can be used as **leg-breakers** to our negative and disempowering internal representations and beliefs. Power questioning is one of the most outstanding tools in shaping a rich and resourceful visual internal representation and forming a set of powerful beliefs within.

"This tool can help reframe both the content i.e., your internal representation of visuals, sounds and feelings and the context i.e., the meaning associated with any experience. This is enough to transform your belief system and your complete personality. All you need to do now is use this amazing tool.

"Let us now see how power questioning, coupled with GDD, can create a fool-proof system that can help you with unlimited transformational vocabulary." Hatim was absorbing all this and nodding vigorously like a teenager having witnessed magic. He exclaimed, "I am getting the hang of it. It's tough but I am getting the hang of it."

Naada softly reinforced, "You must practice these concepts to make them a part of your nature. Remember, repetition is the mother of all skills. You will need a few days to get going but you will need 10,000 hours to master it. I am still pursuing the process myself. The more you live this message, the better the quality of your life is. You also get a better control of your state of mind each day."

The train stopped at a busy junction for a couple of minutes and then moved on.

Naada wrote as she explained.

Reduce unproductive generalization using the leg-breaker questioning technique (LBQ)

Section A

Examples of unproductive generalized statements (external or internal)

1. You must have money to start a business.
2. Nobody understands me.
3. All women are bad drivers.

Word clues and phrases to identify such statements:

1. Must, have to, necessary, requirement, can't, unable, impossible
2. Nobody, anyone, every, always, never
3. All, everybody

TOOL: Leg-breaker questions you ask yourself (corresponding to the generalization statements or phrases in section A above)

1. Must have money? Which business? Says who?

2. Is it true that nobody understands you? Is there at least one person who understands you? How are you measuring understanding?
3. Are you sure all women? Who told you this? Is this absolutely true? Did you get all the facts and figures?

Hatim wrote the above phrases and explained them to Naada until she was convinced that he had got the hang of it. Naada repeated the process with more phrases.

Reduce unproductive deletion using the LBQ technique

Section B

Example of unproductive deletion statements (external or internal)

1. She is a failure.
2. His children are not very bright.
3. He rejected me.

Word clues and phrases to identify such statements:

1. Instances where a verb has been turned into a noun (identity): 'failing' becomes 'a failure' or 'not performing' becomes 'a bad performer' and 'lying' becomes 'a liar.'
2. Vague words such as bright, good, dark, cool, cold, shining, ugly used to describe someone.
3. Verbs that require clarification.

TOOL: Leg-breaker questions you ask yourself (corresponding to the deletion statement or phrases in section B above)

1. How do you know? What did she fail in? Who says so? Has she failed in everything she has done?
2. Compared to whom? What standard are you using? Who are you measuring them against? Bright in what way?
3. He rejected you in what way? What action of his do you term 'rejection'?

Reduce unproductive distortion using the LBQ technique

Section C

Example of unproductive distortion statements (external or internal)

1. He never buys me flowers, so he doesn't love me.
2. My children are driving me crazy.
3. I know you don't want to support my initiative.

Word clues and phrases to identify such statements:

1. Statements that don't add up; the conclusion stated in the second part is based on the meaning attached to the first part.
2. Statements in which one thing causes another.
3. Statements which include an assumption and suggested mind-reading.

TOOL: Leg-breaker questions you ask yourself (corresponding to the generalization statement or phrase in **section C** above)

1. In what way does not buying flowers mean that someone doesn't love you? So in what ways does he show that he loves you?

2. What are they doing to you make you feel crazy? What are your children doing when you choose to go crazy?
3. How do you know? What tells you that? Can you read my mind?

Naada wrote three more bold questions and said, "In addition to the three sections where you can consciously use leg-breaker questions, the following indicators can help you have productive interactions with people. Hatim, the next time you come across opinions, views, statements or information, apply the three- step litmus test for quick validation using the power questioning technique."

1. Is this statement absolutely true and authentic?
2. Is it a positive statement/view/opinion?
3. Is this of use to me or others?

Even if one of the above three don't apply, this opinion is not worth the space of your mind even if the whole world stands absolutely convinced by it.

Chapter 11

Painting the Ten Colors of Excellence

Naada was sipping coffee and Hatim was enjoying his cup of tea. Hatim had known Naada for just eighteen hours but it appeared to Hatim as though he had known her from time immemorial. He put aside his wavering thoughts and asked himself, "What is the bigger purpose in my life that destiny led me to this train to meet this wonderful person?" It was indeed a powerful question. Surprisingly, he wasn't tired of learning, although all his schooling years he had detested theoretical concepts and lectures. He wanted more of what Naada could offer. Naada completed her prayers. Like a committed warrior, she stared right into Hatim's eyes and said, "Now that you have understood that you have in your control the filtering process, how about forming a few empowering beliefs that can make you unstoppable and highly resourceful? This is not a one-size-fits-all approach, but emulating legends who live extraordinary lives is the shortest and easiest way to excellence. Modeling is a very prudent and proven method. We are all naturally attuned to modeling others from the time we are born. We model movements, smiles, languages, styles, accents, habits, behavior, beliefs, values, and so on.

"Much of who we are is a result of the process of modeling. You don't have to reinvent the wheel. Someone has already done it for you. When you need to excel in a field, you will always find a few souls who have made it to the top.

Unless you choose a path that has not been trodden yet, you can safely adopt the path of the few who have excelled climbing the mountain they chose.

"The surprising fact is that, irrespective of the field you opt for, the toppers share many beliefs in common. I wish to share with you a few common empowering beliefs that legends extraordinaire live by, which I choose to emulate. I assure you that each of these ten beliefs are profound and will help you deal with challenges and goals in the most empowered state."

One person with a belief is equal to a force of ninety-nine who have only interests.

- John Stuart Mill

BELIEF 1 – Everything popular may not be right.

"Hatim, for me this is one of the most important and prominent beliefs that prompt me to validate any information, news, view, opinion, rumor, advertisement, value or culture. Many people in our society succumb to practices and rituals just because they are popular among the masses. Thus, we lose the power to exercise our choice and we end up following the crowd. Many people in the world succumb to lifestyles that are defined by a set of people who have managed to make them popular. Anyone going against these norms is made to look and feel like a black sheep in a herd of white ones. Friends, peer and relatives play a great role in creating this feeling.

"The fear of 'what people will say' drives most people into the trap of accepting popular norms that may not be right. Hatim, can you think of a few practices that are popular and not right?"

Hatim spoke immediately as though he was ready with the list. "Dowry, bribe, smoking, alcoholism, junk food, drug abuse, gossip, lying, caste system, racism, and greed." Naada smiled and continued, "These practices are popular and adopted so easily that they are no more seen as detrimental to our way of living. On the other hand, practices such as simplicity, equality, truth, sincerity, integrity and need-based life are considered 'impractical' concepts.

"We are conditioned to accept everything popular and reject everything that is not. Remember Hatim, the next time you hear an opinion, news or view, do not forget to ask yourself, 'Maybe it is popular, but is it right?'"

BELIEF 2 - We have within us all the resources we will ever need.

Everyone is gifted, only few open the package.

- Anonymous

"In 1982, Steven Callahan was crossing the Atlantic alone in his sailboat when it struck something and sank. He was out of the shipping lanes and floating in a life raft, all alone. His supplies were limited and his chances of survival were slim. When the fishermen found him seventy-six days later, he was still alive –much thinner and feeble, but alive. This is the longest anyone has survived a shipwreck on a life raft alone. His narration of how he survived is unbelievably fascinating. He managed to catch fish despite his weak state. He also fixed his solar still, which helped distill sea water and get fresh drinking water.

"But the thing that fascinates the most is this: how did he manage to keep himself going when there was no logical hope, when there seemed no point in struggling and when he was faced with constant defeat? He was hungry, starving and dehydrated. Giving up would have seemed the only sane option. Other than sheer destiny, what makes extraordinary people survive these kind of circumstances? It is what they do with their minds that gives them the courage to keep going and find the guts to carry on in spite of overwhelming odds.

"Many people in similar desperate circumstances give up or lose sanity. 'I tell myself I can handle it,' wrote Callahan in his narrative. 'I tell myself these things over and over, building up fortitude.' Hatim, can you see the incantations Callahan affirmed to himself? He believed that he still had all that he needed to make it through this ordeal. Hatim, whenever you are stuck and your goals seems to be too far away or when your challenges seem too overwhelming, remind yourself with this belief: *I have within me all the resources I will ever need.*

"Every time I have said it, I have always come back to my senses, moved ahead and kept going. I take it one day at a time. Making it through one day is important. I sure have all the resources I need to make it through any ordeal and I do make it. It is important for us to nurture the kind of beliefs carried by Callahan. Belief is the food for our soul and has the potential to make ourselves stronger and our life an extraordinary journey."

BELIEF 3 – Everything happens for a purpose and it is the best for me.

Naada was in a very positive and upbeat state. Each story she shared with Hatim seemed to re-energize her. There were a few passengers from the neighboring compartment who were now keenly listening to Naada, though they didn't make it obvious.

Naada continued, "Hatim, this is a belief that most religions of the world profess and it is a great belief to carry. This is a true story of a 6'4" tall, absolutely charming and handsome hunk. He was wealthy and adored by the masses. He had a loving family too. He was very passionate about horse riding.

"In summer last year, he was enjoying a ride on his horse when all of a sudden, unexpectedly, the horse made a rapid move and he was thrown off its back. He landed neck first. He lost consciousness and woke up in the ward of a hospital, experiencing excruciating pain. He felt as though his head was about to explode. He looked up to find his beautiful wife looking into his eyes.

"Instinctively, he tried to lift his hand to touch her but couldn't. An uneasy feeling went through him and he frantically tried to move his hands and legs, but nothing happened.

"It dawned upon him that the worst thing he could expect had happened. He was paralyzed neck below. He looked up to his wife and with tears in his eyes he said, 'Darling, please let me go and request the doctors to get me to sleep forever. I cannot imagine living like this.' At that very moment, his wife asserted something that changed his focus forever. 'Darling, you are who you are and I love you for that. In fact, everybody loves you for that. I don't know and can't understand why this happened to you of all people, but I strongly believe there is a purpose for what happened. Probably God has chosen you for something much higher.'

"That night, he kept thinking about what his wife said and by dawn he came to terms with himself. 'Yes, it is a fact that when I was bestowed with success and fame, I never questioned it and never asked 'why me?' So, how can I ask that question now? Maybe there is a higher purpose for me to discover.' At that moment, he decided that he would offer himself for medical research so that it would help discover better medication and probably a cure for paraplegic and quadriplegic patients around the world. The moment he made this decision he stood taller than the 6'4" height he had in full health. Do you know who this extraordinary person is? Yes, it is Christopher Reeves, the real life superman.

"We have been sent to this world to face tough situations, trials, challenges and uncertainties. If we crib and complain, we are like the donkey who fell into a dry well. Helpless, the donkey's master tried everything to save it but was unsuccessful. The donkey panicked and brayed louder with every passing minute. Fed up, the master decided to silence the donkey forever by filling the well with mud. When he started dumping mud into the well, the donkey brayed even louder. A few minutes later when the braying stopped, the master peeped into the well and was surprised to see the donkey shaking off the mud from its back and stepping on to it to move up. Slowly and eventually the donkey stepped out of the well alive and kicking. The more we cry and complain, the more unresourceful we become. But if we are convinced that whatever is happening to us in life is for a purpose and for the best, our attitude towards challenges transforms. Like the popular saying goes, when life gives you lemons, make lemonade."

BELIEF 4 – You don't have to be the best to reach the first.

A successful man is one who can lay a firm foundation with the bricks others have thrown at him.

- David Brinkley

"Every year, Australia hosted an 875-kilometer endurance race from Sydney to Melbourne. This was considered the world's longest and toughest ultramarathon. It was a seemingly impossible race that took a week to complete. Only world-class athletes who trained especially for the event took part in it. These athletes were normally less than thirty years of age. Sponsored by big names in sports, the participants were equipped with the most expensive training outfits and shoes.

"In 1983, these top class runners were in for a surprise. On the day of the race, a man named Cliff Young showed up. Everyone thought he was there to watch the event. After all, he was sixty-one years old. He was in overalls and work boots. As Cliff walked up to the table to take his number badge, it became obvious to everybody that he was going to run. He was going to join a group of 150 world-class athletes and run the marathon. Everybody thought it was a crazy publicity stunt.

"But the press was curious. As Cliff took his number and moved towards the pack of runners in their special and expensive racing outfit, the cameras focused on him. Reporters asked, 'Who are you and what are you doing?' 'I'm Cliff Young. I'm from a large sheep ranch outside Melbourne. And yes, I am going to run this race. I got no backers but yeah I can run.'

"Cliff continued, 'See, I grew up on a farm where we couldn't afford horses or four-wheel drives. The entire time I was growing up, until about four years ago when we finally made some money and got a four-wheeler, whenever the storms would roll in, I had to go out and round up the sheep. We had 2,000 sheep across 2,000 acres. Sometimes, I would have to run for the sheep for two or three days. It was tough but I would catch them. I believe I can run this race; it's only five days. I've run for sheep for three days, so I can do it.' It was hard for the media and watchers to believe that this old man could pull it off.

"When the marathon started, the professional runners left Cliff behind in his working boots. The crowd laughed and ridiculed him because he didn't even run properly. He appeared to jog leisurely, shuffling like an amateur. The sixty-one-year-old potato farmer from Beech Forest had started a tough race against world-class athletes. All over Australia, people watched the live telecast and kept praying that someone would stop this crazy old man from running because everyone believed he would die before reaching halfway across Sydney.

"Every professional athlete knew for certain that it took about seven days to finish the race. In order to compete, athletes had to run eighteen hours and sleep six hours. Old Cliff Young did not know this.

"The morning news about the race was aired. People were in for another big surprise. Cliff was still in the race. He had jogged all night to a city called Mittagong. Apparently, Cliff did not stop after the first day. Although he was still far behind the world-class athletes, he kept running. When he got to a town called Albury, he was asked about his tactics for the rest of the race. He said he would run through to the finish. He kept running. Every night he got just a little bit closer to the leading pack. By the last night, he passed all the world-class athletes. By the last day, he was way in front of them. Not only did he run the Melbourne to Sydney race at the age of sixty-one without dying, he also won the first place, breaking the race record by nine hours. He became a national hero.

"The nation fell in love with the sixty-one-year-old potato farmer who came from nowhere to defeat the world's best long distance runners. He finished the 875-kilometer race in five days, fifteen hours and four minutes, not knowing that he was supposed to sleep during the race. He said that when he was running the run, he imagined that he was chasing sheep and trying to outrun a storm.

"When Cliff was awarded the first prize of $10,000, he said he did not know there was a prize and insisted that he had not entered the race for the money. He said, 'There are five other runners still out there doing it tougher than me.' He gave them $2,000 each. He did not keep a single cent for himself. Cliff was a simple humble man, who undertook an extraordinary feat and became a national sensation.

"The 'Young Shuffle' method has been adopted by ultramarathon runners because it is considered more aerodynamic and expends less energy. At least three winners of the Sydney to Melbourne race have known to use the Young Shuffle method to win the race. Now during the Sydney to Melbourne race, almost nobody sleeps. To win the race, people believe they have to run like Cliff Young did – run all-night as well as all-day."

Naada sighed and said, "Hatim, the world strongly believes that you need to be the best to come first. Unless they see you as the best, they will not risk encouraging you. On the contrary, they will criticize and condemn your choice of trying to dare. They see you as a failure as they see the odds stacked against you. No wonder they passionately campaign and dissuade many from giving their best shot. Hatim, you will be surprised to note that eighty percent of the world's population survive, but it is only twenty percent who dare to live and they are the ones who actually run the world. The eighty percent like the comfort of survival and want others to be safe too.

"But for you, this must never be a norm. Every day you have hundreds of ordinary people achieving extraordinary feats. Cliff was neither the best of the lot nor was he formally trained. He also didn't have the equipment needed to create history. But he had one thing for sure: the inner gut conviction that there is no option but to make it to the end. If you noticed, he didn't actually compete with the others. He didn't bother about the people laughing and ridiculing at him. He just did what he was best at and competed against his own best. He won and yet he didn't make a big deal out of it. Hatim, remember this story well. At every stage of life, you will come across people who make fun of, criticize and condemn you for the choices you make. It is up to you keep your calm and take the best from all the criticism as feedback. This will help you derive the hidden treasures of life and make it to the end, which is what matters the most."

Ridicule is the tribute paid to the genius by the mediocrities.

- Oscar Wilde

BELIEF 5 – People are my greatest resource and I must pass the good forward.

If you wish to go fast go alone, but if you wish to go far go along.

- African Proverb

"On a rainy evening, a man saw an old lady stranded on the side of the road. He sensed that she was in need of help. He got off his cycle and pulled up in front of her shining new car. No one had stopped to help her for the last hour or so. Was he going to hurt her? He didn't look safe, he looked poor and hungry. He sensed how frightened she was and said, "Namaste ma'am. My name is Babu and I'm here to help you."

"It was just a flat tire, but for an old lady, that was bad enough. Babu crawled under the car looking for a place to put the jack, skinning his knuckles. In a matter of few minutes, he was able to change the tire. But he had become dirty and his hands were bruised. The old lady couldn't thank him enough for coming to her aid. Babu just smiled as he closed the boot. The lady asked how much she owed him. Babu never thought twice about being paid. This was not a job to him. This was an obligation to help someone in need, and God knows there were plenty of people who had given him a hand in the past. He told her that if she really wanted to pay him, she could opt to pay it forward to someone in need. Babu said, 'And while doing so, think of me.' He waited until she started her car and drove off. He felt good as he headed home, disappearing into the darkness.

"The lady stopped at a small cafe to grab a bite before moving on to the last leg of her trip home. It was a dingy looking restaurant. The whole scene was unfamiliar to her. A young waitress came over with a clean hot towel for her to freshen up. Though she had been on her feet all day, the stress did not erase the sweet smile from her face. The lady noticed the young waitress was poor and was nearing the end of her pregnancy. But she never let the strain and aches change her attitude. She said her name was Solanki. The old lady wondered how someone who had so little could be so giving to a stranger. Then she remembered Babu. After the lady finished her coffee, she paid up with a thousand-rupee bill. Solanki quickly went to get change, but the old lady was gone by the time she came back.

"Solanki returned and noticed something written on the napkin. There were tears in her eyes when she read what the lady had written: 'You don't owe me anything. I have been there too. Somebody once helped me out, just the way I am helping you. If you really want to pay back, do not let this chain of good deeds end with you.' Under the napkin were four more thousand-rupee bills. Well, there were tables to clear, sugar bowls to fill and people to serve, but Solanki made it through the evening thinking about what had happened. How could the lady have known how much she and her husband needed this money? With the baby due next month, it was going to be hard. "When she went home, Solanki couldn't speak much. She broke down in her husband's arms. She then said softly, 'Everything is going to be all right, Babu.' Yes, it was the same Babu who had helped the old lady change her tire."

Hatim was in tears.

Naada continued, "Hatim, remember, people are our greatest resources and we must always pay goodness forward. It is just not about money. It could be a simple act as a smile at the liftman or a pat on the back of the bus conductor or a significant tip to a fruit vendor. You are obligated to do none of these, but doing so makes you a person of value and develops the habit of valuing others.

"Don't be so caught up with achieving your personal goals that you forget the fact that there are many people in this world who are direct influencers on your goals. They may be people whom you know and those you may never meet. Spreading goodness and passing it forward adds more greatness to this world and its existence. This seems like hard work in the initial days but it becomes a contagious habit once it is a part and parcel of your life. Acknowledging that people are our greatest resources helps us develop an attitude of care and selflessness. This allows us to access the master key to nobility and true success."

BELIEF 6 - The meaning of my communication lies in the response.

The most important thing in communication is hearing what isn't being said. The art of reading between the lines is a lifelong quest of the wise.

- Shannon L. Alder

"Hatim, we seldom realize that communication is one of the most powerful tools we possess. We communicate habitually and unconsciously. We seldom communicate for creating outcomes that can add value to our lives or the lives of others. Over sixty percent of what we communicate is sheer rubbish or repetition carried forward from the past. We use communication for reaching out to others and rarely use it to influence favorable action. We are hardly responsible for our communication as we are mostly living in a reactive state. We can never respond when we are reactive. Being responsible for any communication we engage in and its resultant outcome is a sign of completeness in leadership. Communication is power and power can be both used and misused."

Naada resumed after a pause, "There once lived a great mathematician in a village. He was often called by the local emperor for advice on matters of the state. It hurt him very much when the headman told him, 'You may be a great mathematician who advises the emperor but your son is an absolute dud. He does not know the value of gold or silver.' The mathematician asked his son, 'What is more valuable – gold or silver?' 'Gold,' said the son. 'That is correct. Then why is the headman making fun of you, claiming you do not know the value of gold or silver? He mocks me in the presence of others saying that I am a brilliant father who hasn't taught his foolish son anything. This hurts me.' The son replied, 'Every other day on my way to school, the village headman calls me to the banyan tree and, in the presence of the villagers, he holds out a silver coin in one hand and a gold coin in other. He asks me to pick up the more valuable coin. I pick up the silver coin. He laughs and everyone makes fun of me. And then I go to school. This happens every day and that is why they tell you that I do not know which of the two metals is more valuable.' The father was confused. 'Why don't you pick up the gold coin?' he asked his son. 'I am insulted and humiliated every day because of your actions.' In response, the son took the father to his room and showed him a box full of silver coins. Turning to his father, he said, 'If I care for the insults and criticism and pick up the gold coin, the game will stop. They will stop having fun and I will stop making money. By picking up the silver coin I may be dumb in people's perspective, but in reality their response suits me well. Dad, the response of people is most of the time in the control of our communication. We seldom use this power to our advantage. We seldom realize our responsibility in causing wrong responses and keep blaming others for it.' The father patted the son's and said, 'Indeed you have taught me one of the most profound lessons of life. Yes, the meaning of my communication lies in the response I get.'"

BELIEF – 7 - People respond to their representation of reality, not reality itself.

One person's craziness is another person's reality.

- Tim Burton

Naada continued her stories, "A young couple moved into a neighborhood. The first morning, while they were having their breakfast, the wife saw her neighbor hanging washed clothes outside. 'The laundry is still so dirty,' she told her husband, 'Perhaps the lady doesn't know how to wash; she needs a better soap.' Her husband looked on but remained silent. Every day when the neighbor hanged the wash to dry, the wife made the same comments. A few days later, the wife was surprised to see absolutely clean clothes on the line. She exclaimed to her husband, 'Look! Finally, the lady has learnt to wash her clothes properly. I wonder what caused such a drastic change.' The husband calmly replied, 'I got up a bit early this morning and cleaned our windows.'

"Hatim, what we see on the outside depends on the purity of the window through which we look from inside. We are subject to many generalizations, distortions and deletions when we deal with people. These filters make us belittle, ignore or take for granted other people. Our behavior towards them depends largely on the way we have represented them in our mind. When a good friend makes a mistake, it looks like an error to us; when a person we dislike makes a mistake, it looks like a blunder. This is the popular perception. While dealing with people, we must keep aside our past opinions and emotional associations to transact every situation exclusively. We must not be stuck with the map of our past reality. We must do a reality check while transacting with people and circumstances. Failing this, we are bound to have a really narrow view of people and the world. We are easily susceptible to limited internal representations such as the dirty window in the story. We are convinced that our view is right and the outside world is at fault. You may have heard the popular phrase ‘my way or the highway.’ This usually comes from a person who carries a belief that his map is the absolute reality. This is a good belief to carry if you have a process that is open enough to verify before accepting any news or information. Or else you are stuck with an attitude that leads to having a narrow approach and a shortsighted view of both people and circumstances.

“The belief of excellence we are discussing may not appear to be a significant belief to nurture, but trust me Hatim this is a very essential belief, especially when it comes to transacting relationships. Nurturing this belief allows us to empathize with the views of others and learn how to build a rapport with them. Carrying this belief means having more friends, followers and like-minded people in our circle. We will write off fewer people and, in all possibility, we may become a cause of transformation in their lives.”

BELIEF – 8 - People always make the best choice available to them.

He who chooses the beginning of the road chooses the place it leads to. It is the means that determine the end.

- Harry Emerson Fosdick

Naada affirmed, "We are all the time making choices. Be it career, clothes, products or a life partner, every single decision we make is a choice. By nature, we make the best choice at a given time and situation. By accepting this belief, life becomes simpler and understanding the behavior of others becomes easier. I heard a very inspirational true narration from a friend. It went like this: One day, I hopped into a taxi and we took off for the airport. We were driving in the correct lane when suddenly a van jumped out of a parking space right in front of us. My driver slammed his breaks, skidded and missed the other car by just by a few inches. The driver of the other car whipped his head around and started yelling at us. My driver just smiled and waved at the guy in a calm and friendly way. I exclaimed, 'Why did you do that? That guy almost sent us to the hospital.' My driver taught me what I now call The Garbage Law. He explained that many people choose to carry garbage with them, full of frustration, anger and disappointment. As their garbage piles up, they need a place to dump. Sometimes you come in their way and they choose to dump their garbage on you. I choose not to take these dumps personally. I choose to just smile, wish them well and move on. I choose not to take their garbage and spread it to other people, be it at work, at home or on the street. People make the best choices from the options available to them. We don't have to own or feel for the choices others make. The maximum control we have is over the choices we make, while accepting and empathizing with the choices others make. By doing so, I choose not to carry any garbage within me and feel resourceful enough to help offload some of theirs."

BELIEF– 9 - Assume and you will be a perfect fool.

Begin challenging your own assumptions. Your assumptions are your windows on the world. Scrub them off every once in a while or the light won't come in.

- Alan Alda

"Hatim, assumptions are like termites in our tree of beliefs. They are very destructive from the inside and absolutely invisible from the outside till the last stage of breakdown. Weak human minds are a home for assumptions. Transacting and interacting with assumptions is fatal to all the areas of our life. Let me share a story that will give you an understanding of this.

"Yuan was upset and even the first class air-conditioned compartment of the train didn't cool his nerves. He was entitled to air travel but his admin desk had booked him on this train. He opened his bag and took out his geology log book, a rare sight, as he had to complete few tasks. 'Are you from the mining industry, sir?' the man next to him asked. He was staring appreciatively at the strange looking logbook. Yuan looked quizzically at the stranger and nodded in affirmation. 'Engineers like you are responsible for a lot of progress in the country, sir.' 'Thanks,' said Yuan and smiled, as he always found it difficult to resist appreciation.

"The man Yuan was speaking to looked like a simpleton from the village. The man continued, 'You sit in nice offices, execute a few projects and it results in so many big things outside, right?' Yuan smiled at the ignorance of the stranger and said, 'It is not just about a few tasks. There is a lot of thought and process that goes behind it. It is complex, very complex and not for ordinary people to understand.' The stranger responded, 'It has to be. No wonder you engineers are so highly paid.' Yuan remarked, 'Everyone just sees the money we get and no one sees the amount of hard work we have to put in day in and day out. We Indians have such a narrow concept of hard work. Just because we sit in an air-conditioned office doesn't mean that we don't sweat.'

"Yuan explained a few complicated processes of mining and the man listened in amazement, like a child in a zoo. 'You do all these things, sir?' he asked. 'I used to,' said Yuan and paused for curiosity effect. 'But now I am the project manager of a team.' 'Oh!' sighed the man, as if the storm had passed. He continued, 'So your life is easier now because you are a manager.' It was like being told the fire was better than the frying pan. 'My job is to get the project done in time at the lowest cost and with the highest quality. My friend,' he concluded victoriously, 'you don't know what it is to be in the line of fire.' Slowly, the man sat back in his chair, his eyes closed as though he was in deep realization and an intense expression swam across his face. He spoke after sometime with a calm certainty that surprised Yuan. 'I know, sir. I know what it is to be in the line of fire.' He was staring blankly as though no passenger or train existed and it was all just a vast expanse of time. 'There were thirty of us from the 23rd battalion, Punjab Regiment, when we were ordered to the Battle of Longewala in the cover of the night. The enemy was firing relentlessly from the top of a hillock. There was no clue where the next bullet was to come from and whose name was written on it. In the morning, when the firing finally stopped, only four from the thirty of us were alive.' Yuan was shell-shocked. 'You are…?' 'I am Subedar Sushant Singh on duty currently in Kashmir. They tell me I have completed my term and I can opt for a land assignment. But tell me sir, can one give up duty just because it makes life easier?'

"Sushant sat up and with a deep voice and said, 'On the dawn of that capture, one of my colleagues lay injured and open to enemy fire while we were hiding behind a bunker. It was my duty to go and fetch the soldier to safety. But my captain refused me permission and went ahead himself. He said that the first pledge he had taken as a gentleman officer was to put the safety and welfare of the nation foremost, followed by the safety and welfare of the men he commanded. His own personal safety came last, always and every time. He took half a dozen bullets and was killed, but he shielded the soldier into the bunker before he breathed his last. Every morning, as I stand guard I can see him taking all those bullets, which were actually meant for me. I know sir, I know what it is to be in the line of fire.' Yuan looked at the man in disbelief not sure what to say. Abruptly, he closed his logbook. It seemed trivial and even insulting to edit the document in the presence of a man for whom valor and duty was a part and parcel of life – a sense of duty which he had so far attributed only to legendary heroes.

"The train slowed down as it pulled into the station. Subedar Sushant Singh picked up his bags to alight. 'It was nice meeting you, sir,' Sushant said. 'It was an honor meeting you,' Yuan fumbled. He shook hands with Sushant, still feeling ashamed for the assumptions he had made about him. This was the hand that had climbed mountains, pressed the trigger and hoisted the tricolor. Sushant Singh was among the people who put their lives on the line of fire to uphold peace and safety for us and our families. Yuan stood up in attention, and his right hand went up in an impromptu salute. It was the least he felt he could do for a man, who was an unsung hero, like hundreds of other soldiers who made living possible for us."

Naada paused and then began again, "Hatim, assumptions can create havoc in relationships. The human mind is highly assumptive in nature. We tend to pick up a few cues and construct unrealistic stories of people or incidents. Assume and you will be a perfect fool. This is a very powerful belief to have. Fools build assumptions about almost everything they transact or come across. This becomes a second nature to them, making themselves and the others around miserable. Assuming is a stressful job.

"The flight of a lady in the airport was delayed. To while away an hour, she picked up a newspaper and a pack of biscuits. Settling down at the airport lounge, she started reading the paper. A minute later, she heard the crackling of a biscuit. Moving the paper aside she was shocked to see an elderly man munching a biscuit. She was upset with this man. Unable to react or respond, she picked up a biscuit from the pack and started eating it. They ate in turns till the last two biscuits remained. The man picked up one biscuit and smiled. He pushed the last one towards the lady and left. She felt a volcano erupting in her mind. Minutes later, the boarding call was announced. The lady stood up and opened her purse to take her boarding pass out. She was shocked to find her biscuit packet right inside. All the while, she had cursed the old man and was upset with him as she had assumed that he had eaten from her pack of biscuits. In reality, she was the one who had eaten from his pack. But the old man never said a thing. She looked desperately around to apologize but couldn't find the man."

Naada continued, "Hatim, the more a person assumes, the more his mind gets used to it. Though it is hard work to construct unreal images and thoughts, the person gets into an almost compulsive habit of assuming especially the not-so-nice things about people and circumstances. The thing about these images and thoughts is that they seem so real. The mind that assumes is convinced about what it constructs. Many superstitious beliefs are an outcome of assumptions that are strongly planted in a young age and conditioned over and over again. This is a kind of blindness that shields one from seeing and accepting the truth. Whereas, the sane mind always seeks to clarify any ambiguity completely before arriving to conclusions. Be it news, information, gossip or beliefs, always make it a principle in life to verify everything completely before you believe it. Many people spread information without verifying it and such information is what we call 'rumors'. Rumors are mass assumptions that can set individuals and communities against each other for no real reason. Rumors, when accepted by the masses, can create a divide so deep that these are carried forward as truth from one generation to another. In the bygone days, enmity between tribes and nations was predominantly built around assumptions and rumors. The damage assumptions make is just colossal.

"Assumptions are also the primary cause for damaging relationships, be it professional or personal. I have counseled many conflicting couples and I am amazed that the predominant cause of conflict is a bunch of assumptions. When both the partners agree to arbitrated discussions, the assumptions come out in the open and this simple realization gets them back together and stronger. But it takes a while and effort to break down the assumptive constructs in the mind. So keep your mind away from these termites as they can cause havoc inside you and derail you from all goodness."

An unplanned silence took over. Naada was in deep thought while Hatim was looking out of the window trying to hide his emotions. He was feeling embarrassed that he had nurtured an assumptive mind. He understood the fact that most of what he had constructed in his mind could well be untrue. In the screen of his mind, he was running through the people and circumstances in his life and questioning the authenticity of what he thought of them. His dad was one of the subjects of Hatim's contemplation. Hatim was confronted with partial and insufficient evidence with regard to his views of his father. He was unconsciously cleaning his internal frames of representation and making key changes in his core beliefs. He was consciously making a shift from disempowering beliefs to empowering ones. Naada understood the need for this silence and allowed Hatim to be with himself.

It was a pleasant evening and Hatim reflected within, "I certainly did not imagine destiny would unfold thus and a simple train ticket would lead me to such an immense journey. There is a higher power controlling the orchestra of life and I must learn to be led and submit to that power." He gradually got into a deep sleep, while Naada started her prayers.

BELIEF 10 - It is not necessary to understand everything about something to be able to use it.

If you understand everything, you must be misinformed.

- Japanese Proverb

Forty minutes later, Hatim woke up with a startle. Naada offered him a cup of water and he drank it as though he had not seen water for weeks. Once he was settled, he asked, "So what's belief ten?"

Naada was ready, "There is a common belief in the masses that urges people to gain tons of knowledge, best skills and peak attitude before attempting their passion or moving towards a direction in life. Most people invest years in this quest and ultimately the desire for achieving the task dies a natural death. The essence of life is to be in action and keep learning as we go along. We all make mistakes while we pursue our passion. Sometimes these mistakes teach us the most prolific lessons of life. Doing something specific or special for 10,000 hours persistently will make you a specialist in that field. It doesn't mean that you clock 10,000 perfect hours, but it means you must expend your focus, energy and efforts in pursuit of this specialization. Many of those 10,000 hours could have been mistakes and thinking time. Also when you started, you may not have known everything about this field.

"Hatim, I keep thinking of this story of a fourteen-year-old boy who was driven by a passion to do something crazy. He made it happen, at a time when he had no real knowledge and means to achieve his goal. Listen carefully.

"Abayomi was born in Africa, a country plagued by AIDS and poverty. Like most people in his village, his family subsisted on the meager crops they grew. They lived without the luxuries that were considered necessities in the West—electricity and running water. They were living on the edge.

"Their situation became dire in when Africa experienced the worst famine in fifty years. Struggling to survive, fourteen-year-old Abayomi was forced to drop out of school because his family could not afford the twenty-dollars-a-year tuition fee. Though he was not in a classroom anymore, Abayomi continued to think, learn and dream. Armed with curiosity, determination and a physics book that he discovered in a nearby library, he embarked on a daring plan – to build a windmill that could bring his family the electricity that only two percent of Africans could afford. Using scrap metal, tractor parts, old pipes, a broken cycle and blue-gum trees, Abayomi forged a crude yet working windmill. It was an unlikely hand-built contraption that would successfully power four light bulbs and two radios in his family's compound. Soon, news of his invention spread, attracting interest and offers of help from around the world. Not only did Abayomi return to school but he was also offered the opportunity to visit wind farms in the United States to look at the kind of windmills he hoped to build across Africa. This is the moving tale of one boy's struggle to create a better life. The tale of the boy who harnessed the wind is an amazing story; it is a journey that offers hope for the lives of other Africans and the whole world, irrefutably demonstrating that one individual with a belief can make a huge difference. He had no formal education or specialized training but he used whatever he had at hand and made the best of it. Abayomi didn't have a PhD in physics but he applied whatever little he gathered to make a difference to himself, his family and his village. He was an inspiration for the much despaired people of Africa.

"Hatim, we must never get bogged down by the feeling that we are not well equipped or well-educated to make my dream a reality. We are already bestowed with all the necessary potential to achieve our dreams and goals in life. We don't have to wait to get a formal certificate or comprehensive knowhow of a chosen field before taking it up. Abayomi proves this point with what he did for his family. To sum up, you need not know how the internal combustion engine works to drive a Ferrari. You just need to shift your gear and take the beauty for a spin. The only essential thing is to have a dream that will not let you sleep. Once you have that in place, you can go about chasing your dream and learn while you run."

Chapter 12

Dad Unlimited

Sipping coffee, Naada casually began, "Let us now talk about your dad. What are some of the beliefs you have associated with your dad?"

This wasn't difficult for Hatim at all. He started a spontaneous outburst.

"Dad never understood me. Dad didn't have time for me. Dad never allowed me to choose and always dictated things."

"Dad this, dad that…" A small list added up.

Naada had noted down the list. She thoughtfully read aloud the first belief, "Dad never understood me." She then responded with a leg-breaking question. "Never?" To this, Hatim responded, "Well, actually, aahh… Errr… Not never but most of the time he didn't understand me. Actually Naada, I am always blaming my dad. I see that I have generalized, distorted and deleted information about him to myself. I also understand that I have been carrying a whole load of assumptions. It is clear that I am using the same stinking vocabulary again and again and I seem to have gained expertise in it. I know many of my friends who undergo the same turmoil. They are convinced that they are right and their parents are wrong. Over these years, I have nurtured a set of limiting beliefs that have messed up my relationship with my dad. Moreover, I have spent a lot of time, effort and energy nurturing these thoughts and beliefs. This has completely disempowered me; it is of no value to me or to my dad. Shucks! I should have managed this better ages ago. Destiny didn't permit me to meet you or someone else who could put this in my head." Naada intervened quickly "Everything happens for a purpose and is the best for me."

Hatim experienced a very strange chill across his spine. Something in him was transforming in a big way. Many limiting beliefs that he had built, nurtured and carried all these years were crumbling. It was a domino effect and Hatim experienced a sudden surge of lightness and power. It seemed as though a key link to many limiting and negative beliefs was broken. Hatim sat up with a bright face, a light body and unexplainable surplus positivity waiting to be explored and unlocked.

"Naada, the disempowering belief about my dad and my blame-game with him is gone. I have nothing against him now. This is just magical and please pinch me as I can't believe this is happening to me."

Hatim had never imagined that he could ever speak good about his dad. Naada didn't stop at this. She continued, "The conflict with your dad was a blessing. Let us see if you can consciously list out the positive outcomes and good attributes of your dad. For this, you will need to apply the technique of 'emotional disassociation.' Close your eyes and move out of Hatim's perspective to a third party view of your dad. Take your time and express what you see, hear and feel."

Hatim clearly and confidently compiled many beliefs of excellence. He began, "I have within me all the resources I will ever need but I kept blaming my dad for what he didn't provide me. I didn't attempt to understand his map of reality, his world, his challenges and his perspective. I responded to my representation of reality, which may not have been the whole reality. My dad has always been a hardworking man, completely committed to working overtime to keep our family comfortable. I have never seen my dad take a holiday or complain about the tough circumstances he faced. He is my dad by destiny and he is the best for me. He is a blessing and my closest resource whom I failed to reach out to. Most of the good I have is because of the values rubbed off on me by my parents. They have taken care of me when I was in no capacity to fend for myself. My dad was there for me even when I did not ask for him.

"The response I got from my father was based on my communication with him. Most of the times, my interaction with my dad was limited to hopeless conversations with a defeatist attitude. The little I communicated with him was with a lot of negative baggage, distressed body language, distorted internal vocabulary and frustrated emotions. Not only when faced with him, but even when I thought of him, I had the same emotions running in my mind. Had I communicated to him properly and more wisely, I am sure I would have had a better response from my dad. My dad made the best choice available to him when dealing with me. He did his best and I could not see this reality due to the hazy glasses of my mind. I understand now that there was no criticism from him, it was always useful feedback. Just that I did not accept the feedback offered by my parents, especially my dad."

Naada was obviously impressed with Hatim's understanding but she didn't say so. She was amazed at his quick learning capability. Hatim was thinking aloud. Naada did not interfere.

"I am responsible for what has happened so far. This is not the guilt in me speaking but an empowered voice that is ready to make amendments and take charge of transforming my relationship with my dad. And you will be happy to know that I am very confident about my next steps. I can already see clearly, in the new constructs of my mind, that this relationship will certainly transform. I stand committed and I will not give up until I have made this a reality."

Chapter 13

Compass Your Ship and the War is Yours

Try not to become a man of success but a man of value.

- Albert Einstein

Naada was now sort of relieved that the major hurdle was cleared and the last part of what she had to share with Hatim was nearing the fag end. She knew that she had only a few hours before they would part ways; they may not meet each other again. She had to complete the message as this was her passion and mission — enabling people to enable themselves and connecting them with a noble purpose in life. With zeal she began, "Man has been blessed with a special intellect and natural inclination towards the truth of life. We are beings of a higher purpose and not like animals who arrive, survive, reproduce and die. Rather than discovering our purpose in life, we blindly follow what our forefathers did or what the past nations prescribed."

Naada was at her peak state. With an intense expression she said, "Hatim, I can share with you some pointers on the need for discovering your purpose in life and going after them. But the job of discovering the purpose rests on your shoulder. I can't do it for you, you must do it yourself." Hatim was game.

Naada proceeded, "We are complete only when we achieve targets and keep going on the roller coaster ride.

In many countries, there is a sad practice of adhering to the retirement age. Usually people who work in the government sector are asked to retire at the age of sixty-five to sixty-eight years. A big send-off marks this occasion, but seldom do the people practicing this system realize that man is not born to retire but to live till he dies. The essence of living is to strive constantly to add value to one's own life and to the world. Statistics show that people who are declared 'retired' actually lose health, get redundant and have emotional breakdowns; many die early."

"So what is my point?" Naada asked. Hatim was engrossed and had absolutely no clue about what was to come. He was so mesmerized that he was just being present in the moment. He confessed, "I don't know what you are hinting at Naada, but I am all ears."

"We are creatures of direction, beings who need something to aim and run for. This is an instinct within and we behave like warriors seeking and achieving our own battles in life. For those who do not realize this fact, life becomes a misery and they will crib and complain about every challenge that crops up. For sure no human can escape his battles in life. We cannot blame life or the design of destiny for throwing these battles at us. It is our responsibility to accept these challenges and choose those battles that can help us win the war."

Naada continued, "This is a story that can help you begin your journey of being a warrior within. There was once an old Japanese businessman Xu Bing, who built an empire in Thailand. He had business interests in water treatment, heavy earth moving equipment and construction supplies. Barzatin, an engineer apprentice, had to accept Xu Bing as a mentor and work along with him for a period of time.

Though Barzatin was not keen initially, he had no choice but to take up the assignment due to a major contract. Barzatin observed the old man being proactive, positive, enthusiastic and upbeat. As days passed by, Barzatin started adoring Xu Bing and learning from him. They became good friends. At the dinner table one evening, when Xu Bing was in great spirits, Barzatin asked him, 'Mr Bing, what is your age?' Xu Bing gave a naughty look and said, 'Which age?' To Barzatin, this was an unexpected response. He repeated the question assuming that Xu Bing did not understand his question. 'Mr Xu Bing, what is your age?' 'Which age?' Xu Bing said again. Barzatin was completely baffled. Xu Bing clarified, 'I have two ages: one is my biological age which is seventy-six years and I can't do a damn thing about it, and then there is another age.' He touched his heart and said, 'Its eighteen years in here and I have never ever grown older.' Barzatin had a resigned look that seemed to say 'cut this rubbish theory; it is fit only for fairy tales.' However, the awe and respect he had for Xu Bing did not permit him to be candid. He said, 'Mr Xu Bing, with all due respect, I think this is a good concept for motivation, but certainly not real.' Xu Bing quickly responded, 'I don't profess anything that isn't real and non-practical. I can prove what I said to you. You have seen my walking, talking, driving, working, enthusiasm, positivity, hard work, endurance, crisis management, decision-making and other interpersonal and management skills. Aren't my skills an exhibition of youth?' Barzatin agreed. 'Can a man seventy-six years old behave thus?' Barzatin agreed that this was true and these were the qualities that made Xu Bing a great leader, a fantastic role model and a sharp businessman.

"The next logical question from Barzatin was, 'So what makes you feel eighteen within?' Xu Bing was ready with the answer as he lived his message. He bent forward and whispered into Barzatin's ears, 'I don't run behind goals.' This was like a bolt from the blue for Barzatin. All his life, every person Barzatin had come across emphasized the importance of goals. Now, after twenty-seven years of his life, he faced a man who was challenging this popular belief head-on. This was a typical leg-breaking statement for Barzatin. He painfully lamented, 'But Mr Bing, you have your factories, your villas, your big bank accounts, your business, your cars and a whole load of other possessions. Aren't these goals?' 'Of course Barz,' said Xu Bing. 'I enjoy every one of them.' Barzatin was visibly puzzled now.

"Xu Bing waved his hand indicating him to calm down and said, 'Barzatin, I was like you before, weak in listening. You didn't hear me well. I said I don't run behind goals. I didn't say I don't have goals. These are two very different things.' 'So what do you run behind?' asked Barzatin. 'I run behind a vision,' announced Xu Bing. This was a new word for Barzatin. 'What's a vision? I have never heard of this word other than at the optical store.'

"Xu Bing's state changed. His head rose, his body humbled with honor and his voice became firm. 'Barzatin, let me share with you the biggest secret of life. A goal is usually self-oriented where one wants more and more for himself. A goal is want based; and wants never subside, they always grow. When you gain something, you are happy for a while, but in no time the wants increase to the next level of desire. You are seldom content with meager material goals as they are, by nature, greed-oriented. You can never gain lasting happiness with such goals.'

"Xu Bing's posture changed again as he looked up just like Mr Miaggi in the movie *Karate Kid*, and said, 'Whereas, a vision is different as it is a selfless endeavor. A vision is our chief aim in life. It inspires us to work for others and make a difference to a bigger family, other than the one we have at home. It gives us a chance to work for a larger family, seen and unseen. You are focused completely in making a difference to many lives, known and unknown. It is never about I, me, myself. It is always about everyone other than myself. It is 'we' before 'me', always.' The journey towards your vision is exciting and fulfilling. It makes you live in the moment irrespective of the outcome. Many extraordinary people have gone after a vision that was not realized in their lifetime. But these people lived every moment of their lives to its fullest, leaving behind not material things but a legacy for ages to come. For a man who has clarity of vision, any goal becomes meaningful only if it complements his vision. The answer to the 'why' of your goals lies in your vision. Goals become the subsets of the vision.'"

Naada explained, "Hatim, the one who created you and me and enabled us with such perfection and awe did not create us to run behind meager material goals. Thus, material goal is not our prime purpose in life. This is simple common sense. However, we need to achieve a few meaningful goals that ultimately make sense to the vision we decide. Our vision is the path to realize our true purpose in life. It is a channel to give back goodness to mankind for whatever God has bestowed on us. Goals are mere means; vision is the true end value.

"Xu Bing shared this truth with Barzatin, 'By nature, when you run behind goals, goals tend to run away from you.

When you run towards your vision, goals tend to run behind you. Barzatin, I understand that you may not relate to what I share now, but do remember that discovering your vision is the most important aspect of your purpose in life.' Barzatin was waiting to confront, 'Mr Bing, so what is your vision in life?' Xu Bing's state changed again like the sharp and reflective Mr Miaggi. He looked very emotional as he said, 'When I left Japan forty-eight years ago, I had nothing but a ticket to Thailand and a vision. I wished to set up a salt water desalination plant for my village, as we had scarcity of drinking water. This vision is a reality as I speak to you. I never planned to build this empire. All this is an outcome of the passion I had for the vision I believed in. Everything I did was keeping my vision in mind. Even to this day, a chunk of our profits are used to keep the desalination plant at my village running. I will keep doing this till the day I breath my last.' Barzatin was dumbfounded and awestruck. He didn't utter a word till the dinner ended. Still pensive, he thanked Xu Bing for the meal and left. He never imagined that the distinction between a vision and a goal would have such a profound impact on his thinking and direction in life. Barzatin went back to his country and became a social entrepreneur working for the youth and underprivileged people in society."

Hatim was significantly moved and said, "This Xu Bing has left me absolutely inspired. I never ever thought that making a difference to others is a moral obligation and a higher purpose to pursue. I must realign and prioritize many of my goals and direct them towards a worthy vision, which I am yet to define." Naada smiled and said, "Exactly. I will take you through a simple, step-by-step and comprehensive method to define your vision in life and choose goals that align with that vision."

Hatim felt like the chosen one.

"First off, write down the following five power questions.

1. What is it that will make me jump out of bed every morning?
2. What is it that I love to do?
3. What is it that I would do even if I were not paid for?
4. What is it that I would pay and do?
5. What is it that I would do that would allow me to sleep satisfied every night?"

Hatim said, "These questions seem so simple yet they are so powerful. I am able to visualize myself doing some kind of business that involves trading. I can also see that this is a one of the goals I need to achieve but it is not the end." Naada interrupted and asked, "How do you relate to your past, present and future?" Hatim was not sure he understood the question. Naada clarified, "In the space around us, if I were to ask you to physically point to the past, present and future where would you locate them?" Hatim, who now understood the question, pointed to the past behind him, the present below him and the future ahead of him. Naada continued, "You now need to stand up, face the pathway of the train compartment and close your eyes. You have to imagine and visualize you are walking the timeline of your life with the past behind you, the present right where you stand and the future ahead of you. As I keep asking questions, you will express the answers and when done, I will ask you to step forward. You will then take a small step into the future and decide a date. Does this sound simple?" Hatim repeated the whole process and Naada acknowledged it with a nod.

Hatim then stood up and declared, "I am now in the present" Naada tried to calm Hatim's mental state to a normal and relaxed one. She asked, "What are your current goals in life? You may dwell on emotional, financial, mental, physical, relationship and spiritual goals." Hatim was silent for a while and then hesitantly began, "I want to be emotionally fit, financially sound..." Before he could say anything further, Naada said, "Your goals must be defined with a measure of clarity. They should not be ambiguous. Start again." Hatim now had some idea of the framework and began confidently, "I must clear my mind of its baggage, I must make a million dollars soon, I must put on at least four kilos of weight and I must take care of my parents and family."

Naada looked at him without saying a word. Hatim opened his eyes and was puzzled. Naada emphasized, "What you can't measure, you can't improve. You must have absolute clarity of the action you will initiate to make the goals happen or else they will remain in the wish-list. Hatim, I am certain that you can do this if you give it a minute of focus and visualize the goals." Hatim took a deep breath and with a calm mind he pondered the actions he would take to cause worthy outcomes. This time he could visualize a confident person acting on the desired outcomes with a sense of certainty. He slowly but firmly said, "I must define my vision for life in the next one week, I must list out my limiting beliefs and transform them starting today, I must use the new beliefs I have learnt to chalk out a personal and professional plan for the next two years in the next one month, I must read one self-help book every month for which I must buy half a dozen books immediately, I must remain coachable and take up remote coaching and mentoring with you and a few other experts from the field I choose, I must call my parents every day in the first half to check on them and give them quality time, I will not share any of my challenges and adversities with my parents, I must have a twenty-minute daily exercise schedule, preferably at dawn and sleep a minimum of six hours at night."

Naada smiled and said, "Now you are speaking." She said, "Hatim, you missed out the spiritual goals." Hatim responded, "From my childhood, I have no understanding of this aspect as I have never seen my folks being spiritual, except doing rituals of sorts." Naada said, "I understand and I am not expecting you to speak of renouncing the world and taking off to the forest. I am invoking the aspect within you that recognizes that you are the best creation in this universe and you have a higher purpose to live with and die for. You and I have not been created human beings by chance. There is a larger design in our existence and our maker certainly has a unique plan for us, probably as unique as our fingerprints. What if, at the end of the journey of life, we discover that our goals were not the true goals but fake materialistic desires to compete with the possession and power that others flaunt? If we must achieve excellence in the pursuit of any vision or goal, what are the elements we must look for? What are the factors that will give us clarity of purpose and a certainty of direction?"

Naada continued, "Hatim, what's your favorite sport?" Hatim's face lit as he replied, "Soccer."

"So Hatim, if you wish to excel in soccer what are the basic requirements?" Hatim thought for a while and said, "Passion and knowhow."

Naada responded, "Excellent! You got two out of three. You are almost there." She sketched again and said, "Consider the following popular triangle of success adapted by most human beings naturally. All goals begin with a burning desire to achieve an outcome. Secondly, we are naturally compelled to acquire all the knowledge about the goal. Thirdly, we tend to develop competitive skills related to this goal by investing many hours of practice."

Hatim nodded in agreement.

Popular Success Triangle

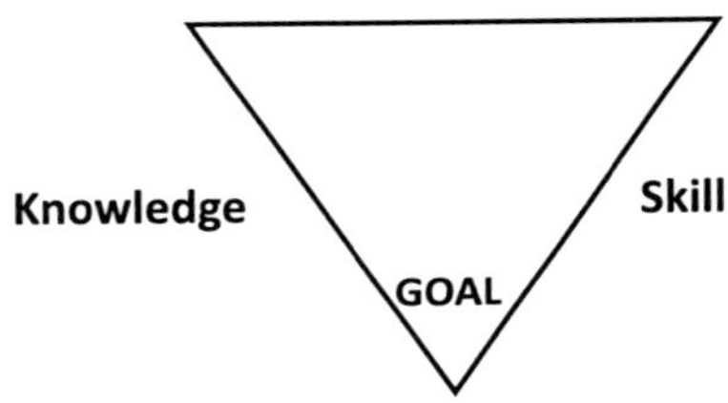

Burning desire to excel in soccer

"How do we ensure that this is a quality goal and aligned to our purpose in life?" Hatim didn't have an answer and looked on in anticipation. Naada continued, "If the triangle has to stand tall and stable, the foundation must be rock solid; it doesn't look so here. Let us consider one more example in which the goal is to excel in making money. Let us take the case of Sid, an ambitious graduate engineer from a reputed university in South India. He had a clear desire to make a lot of money by gaining expertise in information technology (IT). With this money, he wanted to take good care of his family, have an expensive lifestyle and travel around the world. So he grabbed the first opportunity that came his way and took up training in IT security and hacking, an upcoming domain in the early nineties and a highly sought-after area. Being a topper, he learnt fast and became a recognized security expert and an ethical hacker in a year. At a dinner during an IT event, Sid met his good old friend Som, who had also pursued a similar career. Som hailed from a middle-class family as well, but now owned top-end cars and other branded gadgets. When Sid visited Som's house, he was shocked to see that Som's standard of living was no less than that of a top management executive. Curious to know how he achieved all this, Sid asked him the secret to his financial success. Som gave him random answers that did not satisfy Sid. Sid met Som regularly and they become thick friends. One Sunday, Som asked Sid if he was interested in making some extra money. Sid agreed immediately. Som took Sid into confidence and disclosed to him that the project they were involved in was a highly sensitive job and required utmost confidentiality. Sid signed a non-disclosure agreement and a contract. For the first time, Som introduced Sid to the world of hacking for quick gains. The payouts were ridiculously high for a part-time job. Sid was a bit hesitant initially, as he knew that it was an unethical practice. But the advance payment check, which was more than his annual salary, got his knee buckling. He dug his teeth deep into the bait and in a matter of few years, he became one of the wealthiest and respected people in his hometown. He achieved the financial goals he had set for himself."

Sid's Success Triangle

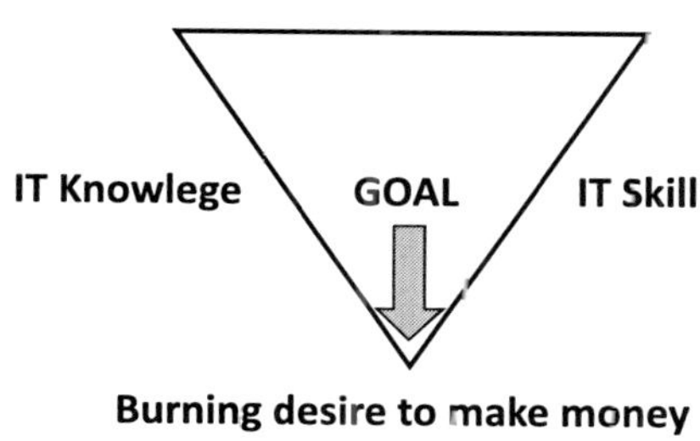

"Hatim, what do you think of Sid?" Hatim looked disgusted and said, "He is a criminal of the first order and if caught he will be behind bars for life." Naada asked, "So what's missing Hatim? Why do Sid, Som and many people like them, after investing their efforts in school, college and university and obtaining a righteous job, succumb to wrong practices?" Hatim pondered for a while and then replied, "Probably they didn't get the right kind of mentoring to differentiate the right from the wrong." Naada said, "Yes, they didn't get enough support to their knowledge, skill and burning desires. They didn't acquire the basic human values or principles shown below."

True Success Representation

"The important dimension of true values is mostly missed out in our society and environment. Values are the compass to our ship of life. A ship is a gigantic machine that has the capability and power to sail the roughest seas. However, without a working compass the mammoth ship is just a big piece of nothing. The importance of basic values should be much publicized and marketed. Values such as truth and honesty are spoken of but they are not demonstrated in real life situations. Unfortunately, there is a massive vacuum in understanding the meaning of principles and values.

Key values such as sincerity and integrity are just concepts found in books and not practiced and used in the real world. This is a hidden generalized belief in itself. Advertisements, movies, promos, news and the education system seldom exhibit these values in action. On the contrary, aspiring for more and the need for flaunting brands have promoted greed, pride and jealousy as a way of life. The notion that respect comes from money and power is another popular generalized belief.

"I was once interacting with a sales team of a very large corporate house in India. When I began the topic of honest sales, I faced severe resistance from the participants. They refuted the concept saying that their managers and other higher authorities in the organization pushed them to sell by hook or crook. The managers only wished to see sales targets being met. They were not concerned about the authenticity of the transaction and the values practiced. However, on the contrary, most organizations boast and make tall claims that they run value-based business practices. Unfortunately, the values they claim to follow are displayed only on their branding and marketing collateral and website. They are seldom practiced on ground. So how would people like Sid and Som ever consider basic values such as sincerity and integrity as crucial aspects to their inner being and consider them critical to any decision or action they take? Scary right? Standing by the truth, sincerity and integrity will unfold our true designed destiny and purpose of life. If you go back to Xu Bing, he had a wonderful grounding in righteous values – especially that of vision orientation and sincerity to the cause of making a difference to the people of his town. He did own many materialistic possessions but he was not driven or obsessed by them. He controlled them and did not allow them to control him. He considered them as mere means to the end and not the end itself. The journey towards your vision and goal becomes more fulfilling and the outcome more meaningful if you commit to a few basic values and stick to them without a compromise."

Hatim was waiting to share something. It was evident on his face. Naada paused for a while and allowed him to speak.

"Naada, I have always seen both my mom and dad making a huge difference to the lives of orphans, beggars and the needy. I remember vividly how my mother empowered a few beggars by encouraging them to quit begging and take up small jobs. Today, the beggars have their own homes, their children go to school and the entire family is transformed in their own little ways. I have also seen my dad give his belongings to those in need, although he himself was in a lot of debt and faced difficult times."

"I have unconsciously picked up the trait of having a soft corner for the less privileged people. Somewhere in the back of my mind, there lies a vision to make a difference to this section of society. All this while, I had assumed that I had to first make it big and then think of doing something for others. However, listening to Xu Bing's story, I now have a vision to support families who can't fend for themselves and educate the needy youth of our society. In short, I want to give fish to those who can't fish and teach fishing to those capable of fishing. I have decided that this vision need not wait anymore."

Naada smiled and said, "I am glad you are talking about your dream vision before setting any goals, as this is a sign of greatness to come. Can you pen down your vision, Hatim?"

Hatim thought for a while and wrote, "I MUST live to work hard and make a difference to the youth of our city and nation at large. Through these youth, I MUST work with the underprivileged people of my town and provide food, education and employment. I MUST set up small teams and centers in the slums that can empower students. I MUST also start a venture that will channelize food provisions to highly deserving families. I will hold tight to the values of sincerity to God and empathy to people."

Naada was elated with the declaration and said that Hatim's statement was inspiring and she had never made a statement anywhere close to this. She was in a state of gratitude for having a mentee like Hatim.

Chapter 14

THE UMBRELLA OF LIFE

We all die. The goal isn't to live forever; the goal is to create something that will.

- Chuck Palahniuk

"Hatim, as you spoke about the importance of intending the vision first, let me share with you a visual that will remind you to maintain constancy while seeking your purpose in life. Consider the visual of an open umbrella, which represents our life. The arch-like canopy on the top is the most important part of the umbrella and it represents your vision, purpose or end goal in life. This is your primary aim, dream or vision for a long time to come. The central stick of the umbrella, which controls and allows a firm grip, is comparable to our core values that need to be held tight and cannot be compromised, especially during rough weather. The spokes that help the umbrella canopy open up and spread out wide can be compared to the various means, tasks or goals that align with the vision and support it."

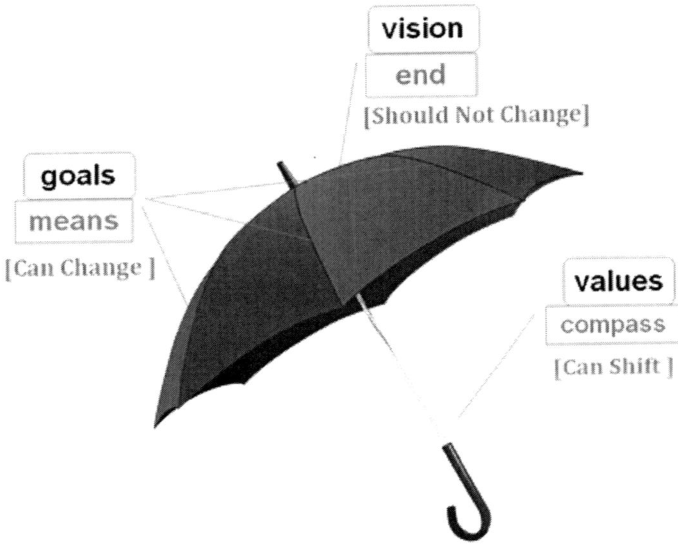

Hatim was impressed by this pictorial representation and said, "I will carry this umbrella in all walks of my life. This serves as a quick and handy reminder."

Naada said, "Just to reinforce: all goals fall under the areas of our life. Remember we spoke about the areas of life while discussing habits and beliefs?"

Hatim nodded in the affirmative and listed out the six important areas of life.

1. Spirituality (God, Vision, Purpose, Mission, Service, etc.)
2. Me (Identity, Skills, Emotions, Discipline, Planning, etc.)
3. Family (Important Relationships, etc.)
4. Wealth (Assets, Finance, Money, Worth, Network, etc.)

5. Health (Fitness, Vitality, Food, Schedule, etc.)
6. Others (Friends, Relatives, Neighbors, Society, Country, etc.)

Naada continued, "You can chalk out your goals under the above six headings while checking on your vision in life and the core values you have centered your life around. It is advisable to write your goals and do a periodic check on them. Can you pick a **Truly Important Goal (TIG)** to run a timeline walk and validate the goal with a reality check?"

Hatim nodded and said, "I will choose a financial goal that complements my vision. I MUST build a business in the field of non-perishables that can give me an income of about two hundred thousand a month. I will double the income in three years. My commitment towards my vision will be a straight twenty percent of the profits."

Naada was impressed but didn't express this again. She said, "Stand up now and close your eyes." Hatim obeyed instantly. She continued, "Take a deep breath and point in the direction of your past and future."

Hatim pointed to his past behind him and his future right ahead. Naada now instructed, "I will make you physically walk a timeline of your financial goal for the projected period of the next three years with your eyes closed. You can apply this technique to validate any goal you wish to take on. You will start from your current location, which relates to the present day and date. You will step forward when I prompt you. Every step will take you forward by six months. You will pause for a while at each of the six stops and express the following:

1. Visualize all that is happening around your TIG on that date.

2. Express aloud what you see and hear about your TIG.
3. Express your emotions and indicate their location on your body."

Two more people in the train compartment joined the silent audience. They pretended not to be watching but they were completely engrossed in observing Naada coach Hatim. Meanwhile, Hatim was absolutely unaware of the surroundings. It seemed as though he didn't care about the audience.

Hatim began, "Today I see that I have decided on my financial goal of starting a business. I see myself pretty confused and uncertain. I can see a lot of resistance from my immediate family and relatives. My friends are not sure of my success but they are supportive. I have a mild emotion of confidence and this feeling is around my abdomen." Naada firmly said, "One step forward." And Hatim promptly announced what he saw in the next six months. "This day, I see that I have made a start and the hard work of the last six months is paying off. I have developed a network and I can see myself progressing. I have bagged a few orders and it looks like I am in the line of building construction. I still have no significant confidence and the feeling is around my abdomen." Naada said, "Move a step forward."

Hatim pronounced the date after the next six months and detailed what he saw, "I can see that my family is supportive of my decision to venture into this business. I am making enough and more money to take care of myself and contributing a substantial amount to my family. I am working overtime and enjoying it as well. I am supporting a friend by giving him a job in my firm. He is assisting me in most of what I do.

The future looks bright and I am experiencing victory. The feeling of strength and boldness is around my chest." After taking six steps, Naada made Hatim turn around open his eyes and see his three-year timeline with a disassociated perspective. Hatim made a few suggestions and changes, which made quite a lot of sense. He had clarity and a roadmap to tread. Naada proceeded to do a few more validations on Hatim.

"What is your current environment, the place you work the best, the world you want to explore, the kind of home environment apt for you in achieving your TIG, the kind of people you prefer to work with and the time of the day you get the best focus to crack your goal?" With his eyes closed and standing in attention, Hatim responded, "I currently do not have a conducive environment apart from this train compartment and a fantastic coach to help me (Hatim smiled), but I guess I prefer a bright and open working space with greenery around. I work the best when I am both alone and in teams. I would like to explore working with people from different walks of life, especially people from the West. I would love to have a small, minimally furnished and well-lit home. I like people who are happy-go-lucky and intellectuals, both being light souls. I work best from 6 a.m. to 8 a.m. followed by 11 a.m. to 2.30 p.m. and post 8 p.m. for an hour." Naada was continuously noting down this information under the heading ENVIRONMENT CHECK.

Naada then asked, "Does your current behavior and identity support your financial TIG for the next three years? What do you do to make life fun and interesting? What do you get upset with again and again? What do you say about your goal habitually? How do you walk when you are engaged in your TIG? How do you talk (tone and words used) when engaged with the TIG? How do you feel when engaged with the TIG? What kind of a person are you and how do others describe you? How do you picture yourself? What in the above needs a complete shift?"

With eyes still closed, Hatim answered, "My current behavior certainly does not support my financial TIG but the change I have committed to in my behavior will help me achieve it. I must be in constant connect with people and see a turnaround in their lives. I get upset with my incapability to manage time – you have to help me with this. I use words and sentences that create absolutely no feeling of confidence in the completion of my goals. So this needs a U-turn. I walk with low energy, enthusiasm and pace. I identify myself as an unplanned, not serious and easygoing person in need of external motivation, validation and help. Others usually identify me as a multi-talented individual able to take on challenges and win. Basically, I must change a few areas and I will be fine." Naada noted down this information under the heading BEHAVIOR CHECK.

She continued meticulously, "What are the skills that complement your financial TIG? Do you know someone who has a skill you wish to acquire and how will you learn this? What do others say about you when asked what you are good at? What actions would you take up immediately?"

Hatim answered slowly but with certainty, "I do have some of the skills required as I hear this often from my friends. Skills I think I have now are: being bold and fearless in communicating and the ability to take risks. I can also speak to strangers. I have the capability to accept failures as stepping stones and move forward. I also have a proactive nature.

The skills I lack and need to acquire are: financial and business planning, daily task planning, learning tools such as Excel, the habit of reading, team building and management, understanding customers' perspective and saying 'no' when it needs to be said. I know a few people I can reach out for help immediately. Naada wrote down SKILL CHECK.

She continued, "What are the core beliefs and values you carry that complement your financial TIG? Where did you acquire these values? Who are your role models? Are you willing to make changes in your values hierarchy if it needs to align to the vision and the financial TIG you have?"

For the first time in this exercise, Hatim looked stumped. He was clueless about what his values were. He struggled to think and was going nowhere. He looked at Naada and nodded in the negative.

Naada pulled out a sheet and handed it over to Hatim and said, "Pick your top three values from this list that can impact your financial TIG. There are over 400 values, but to make it simple I have picked the top few from which you can choose your top three values. Values are our core beliefs that specifically help us in guiding the goals we choose. We stand for and uphold our values without a compromise. We seldom demonstrate any behavior or habit that transgresses our value system. All human beings live by values but they are seldom aware of them. The typical indication of values usually highlighted in our vocabulary are words such as 'right' or 'wrong', 'must', 'should', 'must not', and 'should not'. Values are an integral part of our existence and are nurtured beliefs that can become convictions.

"While you have agreed to model the ten beliefs of excellence, you already have a good number of your own learnt and adapted core beliefs you can leverage on. These core beliefs or values are almost like your DNA and are a part of your unconscious system. You have learnt and lived by them all your life. They are the reflection of the character of your being. While others would be able to identify the values you live by very easily, you may grapple to identify them. But I want you to go through this exercise that will give you clarity of your top values and support you in achieving your financial goals while aligning with your vision in life with no compromises made. The thing about values is that the entire list seems good and relevant. We all agree with the values but we need not necessarily be practicing them or counting them in our top three. The purpose of this exercise is not to throw this list out of the window, but pick our top three values from them that can give the best momentum to a specific goal we have decided. This list can remain with you to be reviewed periodically. Sometimes we will need to consciously adopt a value to make significant shifts in an area of our life. I can share an example with you to show how knowing our values and making small changes can impact the different areas of our life.

"There was once a tea stall owner Bika who was running a hand-to-mouth existence. He was spiritually well-balanced, his relationships were good and he was very healthy but he suffered in one area – his family was in conflict with him. No matter how hard he tried, he was not able to overcome the differences with his family and was under quite a lot of pressure due to this. The importance he gave to his family was below the norm. One evening, Bika was discussing this challenge with a very close friend Rasi. Rasi asked Bika what he valued most in his life. Bika said that faith in God was the highest purpose of his life followed by his trust in friends, his hobby of pottery, being content with what he had and compassion to his maternal relatives.

"If you observe, Bika was spelling out his current values. Rasi, a wise man, suggested to Bika that he consider holding on to being content in all aspects except in the area of making wealth. He advised Bika to have a short-term plan to focus on his business and aim at doubling it. Rasi also emphasized that Bika should spend one full day during the weekend exclusively with this family. After a long conversation and debate, Bika agreed to get accountable with business, committed to growth and also spend quality time on weekends with his family. This was a shift in values, which reflected in a natural change in his behavior. He invested more time and focus on business development. This called for cutting down his hobby time and time with friends and reducing his visits to maternal relatives.

"In the next few months, Bika's income doubled with the addition of a snack joint near the tea stall. His sons' grades got better as he spent more time during the weekends at home. Over the next year, Bika moved his business to a better locality where he opened a south Indian restaurant, which was soon running packed tables. He could afford a better house. His family was completely thrilled with whatever was happening. The good part was that Bika also got back to his pottery hobby and was able to support many of his relatives who were not very well off. So Hatim, can you see how important it is for us to keep track of our values all the time? Any imbalance in any of the areas of our life is an indication that some of our values have taken a backseat and they need a relook and reprioritizing. While we may feel that all the listed values are equally important, we must stand up for the top three and stick to them for a significant time. We must also review them once in a while. Hope this has given some ground for contemplation, Hatim."

Hatim beamed and said, "Wow, it couldn't have been explained any simpler, Naada. I am able to relate to the aspect of values being my core beliefs and their immense influence on the goals I have. This is one area I will constantly work on and I am confident that in due course I will be able to gain familiarity with values and effectively manage them. Let me take up this values list and pick my three top values that can influence my financial goals."

Naada indicated to Hatim to pause and said, "Before you go into the values, have a look at this data I have captured from your timeline walk for the financial goals." She handed over the environment check, behavior check and skills check list documented during Hatim's timeline walk. As Hatim looked through the list, Naada said, "You must be aware of your preferred environment, behavior and skills as you go through your values. While you chose a value that compliments your financial goal, you must also look at its impact on the environment you will work in, the behavior you will need to hold on to and the skills you need for achieving the desired financial outcome." This made a lot of sense to Hatim.

Environment Check

- I prefer a bright and open working space with greenery around.
- I work the best when I am both alone and in teams.
- I like people who are happy-go-lucky and intellectuals, both being light souls.

- I work best from 6 a.m. to 8 a.m., 11 a.m. to 2.30 p.m. and post 8 p.m. for an hour.

Identity and Behavior Check

- I must be connected to people and turn around peoples' lives.
- Others usually identify me as a multi-talented cheerful individual.
- I get upset with my inability to manage time. [area to work on]
- I use words and sentences that show my lack of confidence. [area to work on]
- I identify myself as an unplanned, not serious and easygoing person. [area to work on]
- I walk with low energy, enthusiasm and pace. [area to work on]

Skill Check

- I am bold and fearless in communicating even to strangers.
- I have the ability to take risks and accept failures as stepping stones.
- I lack and need to acquire skills in financial and business planning and daily task planning. [area to work on]
- I have to learn Excel, reading, team building, management and understanding others. [area to work on]
- I need to learn to say 'no' when it needs to be said. [area to work on]

Value list

1. Achievement	2. Independence	3. Steadfastness
4. Caring	5. Justice	6. Tolerance
7. Compassion	8. Love	9. Truth
10. Physical courage and courage of conviction	11. Moderation	12. Assertiveness
13. Detachment	14. Obedience	15. Challenging work
16. Excellence	17. Peace	18. Confidence
19. Faithfulness	20. Power	21. Courtesy
22. Friendship	23. Reliability	24. Determination
25. Health	26. Responsibility	27. Risk
28. Honor	29. Self-discipline	30. Flexibility
31. Generosity	32. Respect	33. Enthusiasm
34. Helpfulness	35. Self-esteem	36. Faith in God
37. Humility	38. Time	39. Forgiveness
40. Integrity	41. Trust	42. Gentleness
43. Kindness/ empathy	44. Wealth	45. Being content
46. Loyalty	47. Beauty	48. Accountability
49. Modesty	50. Cleanliness	51. Family
52. Orderliness	53. Consideration	54. Knowledge
55. Personal growth	56. Creativity	57. Mercy
58. Purposefulness	59. Pleasure	60. Thankfulness/ Gratitude
61. Religion	62. Recognition	63. Trustworthiness
64. Security	65. Dignity	66. Wisdom

Top three core values I will carry to accomplish my financial goals

New Top Three Values	Environment Check	Identity and Behavior Check	Skill Check
1. Accountability How I will leverage this value in the three checks	Look for people who have similar values and operate with transparency, be accountable to God, purpose, client and team	Be task-oriented, objective and have robust financial discipline	Learn Excel, business planning, daily scheduling and business communication
2. **Independence** How I will leverage this value in the three checks	Will not accept blame, blame others or complain, give flexible time for team but emphasis on fast turnaround	Strong decision-making, taking higher risks, confident, proactive and hardworking	Leadership skill development, disciplined mentoring
3. **Family** How I will leverage this value in the three checks	Will not engage family in my business, will not work from home except late at night, will engage in such a way that family supports me	Communicate frequently and lead the family, be gentle and fun loving with them, will not express my challenges to them	Listen to family when they express, be non-judgmental of dad and take everybody along

Looking at the information captured, Naada was thrilled beyond measure but she did not express this to Hatim. She explained, "Hatim, you will have to adopt a similar method to validate all your goals while running a check on the environment, identity, behavior and skill they demand. Finally, make conscious choices of the values you need to stand by to make these goals meaningful and easier to fulfill. You may experience an overlap in all these aspects, which is a natural progression and is perfectly fine. Once you have completed this exercise with each goal, compile all the goals, values and data you have. The summary will give you a roadmap for the timeline you have allocated. You can choose to define your roadmap for a year, three years, five years and so on. Simplify the roadmap and pin it up in the format you understand as a reminder to yourself. After all, we are beings who tend to lose focus while on a journey and slip away from our own decisions and commitments. The metaphor of a highway ahead of us with milestones and sign boards is such an apt and constant reminder. We must not randomly drive anywhere we feel like. Though most of the landscape we see on the journey is attractive and worth exploring, we stick to the highway and keep looking for the milestones and signboards to ensure that we are on the right track, towards the right destination. Hence, a roadmap is a very important tool to have. This may seem tedious but in reality it is simple and is a natural way to assess how we have achieved our goals in the past. We have to do the whole ritual in a more informed and conscious manner. As a very powerful and old saying of the prophet goes, 'Tie your camel and trust in God.' The process of setting vision, goals, values and chalking a roadmap is like tying the camel. It is our duty. The rest involves the unfolding of our destiny through the choices we make. It is in the few moments of invaluable decisions we make that our destiny unfolds. Had you not made the decision to take this train, we wouldn't have met and I would have lost an opportunity to mentor a coachable vagabond."

Naada gave a full smile for the first time. Hatim was in deep contemplation as he nodded his head. Naada sketched something again on a paper. "Hatim, we are all limited by one of the greatest resources – time. We all have the same number of productive hours in a day, month and year. This asset must be used judiciously. Time is an external entity that we cannot control directly. However, we do have control over our own focus. A laser beam is nothing but light that is converged, focused and amplified. This focus makes the laser beam so powerful that it can cut through the hardest of substances.

"You need to allocate control and focus on the TIGs you have defined. Everything else then falls into a routine. The first sketch shows how people get deluded by seemingly urgent goals and spend over eighty percent of their focus and time on them. They ignore or procrastinate the TIG that they are supposed to go after. They achieve very less in a lot of time. At the end, they wonder why they worked so hard and yet did not end up with anything big. The key reason for their low results is low focus on the TIG and nothing else.

"Sketch two shows how the extraordinary few people focus eighty percent of their productive time on the TIG. When they plan, they always prioritize. The TIG occupies eighty percent of their day. At the start of every day, they ask themselves an important question: what are the tasks I need to focus on that will help me accomplish my TIGs fast? When these people get sucked into a routine, they are conscious of the fact that this is not the TIG domain they need to invest time in. Hence, they pull themselves out of the rut quickly.

This is why the extraordinary few are successful in achieving their TIG in the timeline they had allocated for themselves earlier. There is no magic in this whatsoever."

1. **How ordinary people get less in more time**

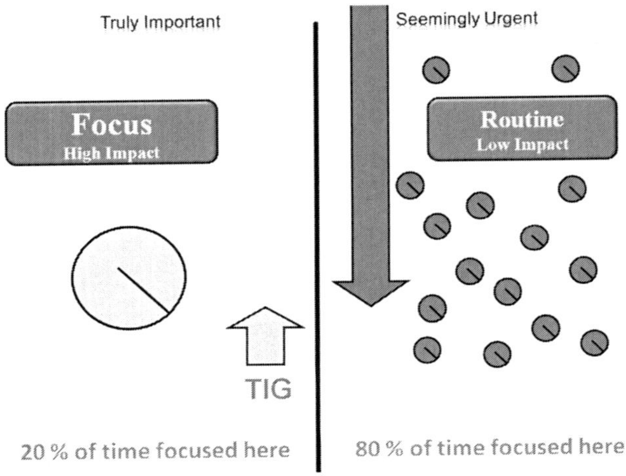

2. **How extraordinary people get more in less time**

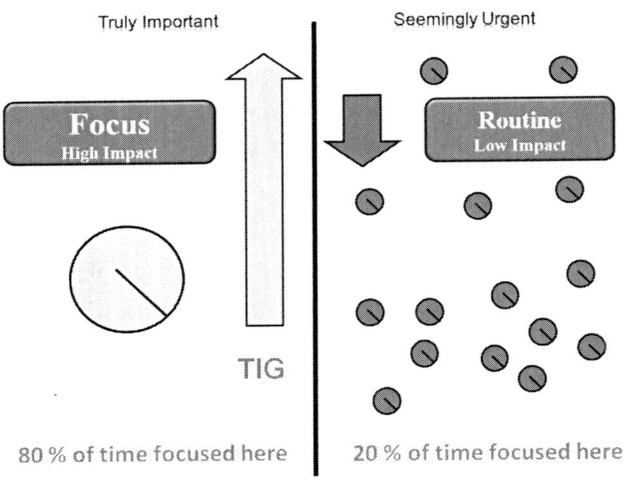

Chapter 15

DIAL WITHIN

"Hatim, do you wish to speak to your dad?"

Hatim was on the phone before Naada completed her sentence. "Mom, it's me." His mother mumbled something and asked Hatim where he was and how they could get in touch with him. She was sobbing uncontrollably and in broken words she said, "Your dad has left home and hasn't come back for the last nine hours. We are in a shock and don't know what to do." Hatim's mother then broke down badly. Hatim couldn't believe what he heard. He felt a strange rush of blood around the back of his neck. His ears changed color from whitish to almost red. Naada sensed that Hatim was up for his first major challenge and she was not very surprised about it.

Whatever he had learnt in the last two days seemed to vanish from his mind for a moment. He consciously gathered himself, "Everything happens for a purpose and it is the best for me." As he spoke to his mother, strong statements and visuals popped in his head. "The meaning of my communication lies in the response," his inner voice prompted him. He could also visualize his mother gathering strength and hope and not panicking. This visual gave him the courage to say, "I am taking the next train back and I will see you the day after, mom. I promise everything is going to be fine."

"I have within me all the resources I will ever need," he told himself. He visualized himself taking charge of the situation at home and his family being relieved with him around. A few more words of assurance spontaneously spurted out of Hatim's mouth and the cell phone lost connection.

Naada spoke to Hatim at length before he got off the train. She reinforced all the information she could. They parted ways by exchanging numbers. Hatim felt a strange immeasurable loss and was a bit uncertain if he would ever see Naada again. He watched as the train left the platform and Naada's silhouette disappeared.

A different challenge was brewing in Hatim's mind. Questions such as 'why did dad do this?', 'where could he be?', 'am I the cause?' and 'what if he is dead?' came to his mind one after another. Mixed feelings of guilt and remorse bombarded him. But this time it was certainly different. He was conscious and aware of the questions, sentences, patterns, the internal habituated vocabulary, the visuals and all the old rituals. He said to himself, "Hatim, reframe your internal conversation and visualization to suit your prime focus in life. You must attend to this emergency fast and get back to focusing on your TIG. You must aim for a resourceful state all the while during this battle. This is a challenge that will help you test your newly acquired knowledge. It is a ground for you to test all that you have learnt in the last thirty-six hours over a distance of 2300 km. I MUST plan the way I am going to handle this challenge and come out successful, while taking charge of the situation and not allowing my family to panic."

It was 8.45 p.m. and the return train chugged out of the Nizamuddin Station in Delhi. It was a going to be a long journey back to Bangalore. Amidst many thoughts and plans, Hatim's heavy eyelids closed almost the same time his head touched the pillow.

Chapter 16

War Zone

The two days in this train were the most difficult days that Hatim had spent, not because he was alone or worried about his father and his family, but because he wanted to put all that he had gained into practice. He was in a helpless state between his old habitual negativity and the conscious efforts to reframe his thoughts and visuals to create and recreate resourceful states. The more he worked within, the more familiar he got to with the ways and thinking patterns of the extraordinary. He couldn't help but remember Naada for her selfless contribution to a stranger like him without any strings attached. This was all the more reason for his commitment towards his own transformation. To Hatim, the world now looked completely different. He did not feel being a part of the crowd anymore. The petty gossip, complaints and casual talk he used to be engaged in earlier did not make any sense to him. His past was not a venue of regret and blame, but a platform for learning. The present was a basket full of opportunities waiting to be explored through the unlimited potential he had discovered. The future was a clear white canvas calling him to innovate with the best of colors and discover the destiny in store. He was ready for life.

The train pulled into the same station he had boarded a week ago. But it was a completely different Hatim who got off the train that day. He jumped into an auto and headed straight home. His heart was calm and mind focused on the fact that he had to manage both his state and the family, especially his mother. He empathized with her in his mind as he realized that the twenty-seven years of his mother's married life were laced with a series of challenges. She was a warrior of sorts and had conquered the challenges head-on.

He paid a lot of extra money to the old auto driver much to his surprise. The driver sat upright, smiled with tears swelling in his eyes. "Thank you, my son," he said. Hatim's vision of making a difference to people had already begun.

His sister ran towards him like a helpless girl running away from the darkness towards the tiniest light of hope. She sank into his arms sobbing uncontrollably. Tears of joy were mixed with overflowing sorrow. Hatim gave her the time and space to cry her heart out. Once she had calmed down, he looked straight into her eyes and said, "I promise everything is going to be all right and I need you to stand strong by me." Shajr nodded in the affirmative. They both walked to the front door. Hatim's mother fell into his arms and wept. He held her firmly and patted her back gently as he unconsciously said, "Mom, everything happens for a purpose and it is the best for us." Hatim's brother was in hostel and was not aware of all that had transpired over the past week. Hatim wanted to keep it that way.

The outburst helped mother and daughter let out their painful pent-up emotions. It helped them a great deal and they started to speak slowly. They narrated the episode of his father missing after a strange phone call from someone called Rudra. He had left the house at 9 p.m. saying he had an important meeting and would return in an hour and a half, but he never came back.

Hatim had a shower, opened his father's cupboard and went through it completely. He found a diary, a telephone book and some documents. He opened the diary and browsed through it. He stopped at one section where the word 'hopelessness' was highlighted, scribbled in his mother tongue script. He read the section and it translated thus:

"Today is December 20, 1991 and I have a hopeless feeling about Hatim as he has become rebellious. I love Saudh a lot but I love and respect Hatim beyond imagination, although he is not my son. This fact is something even my wife doesn't know. We lost our eldest child during birth. With the help of the hospital nurse Gracy, I took a new-born baby as our son and named him Hatim. He had lost his mother the day he was born. He belonged to a very poor family who were in dire need of money. They had no means to take care of Hatim. I did not get a chance to see them for obvious reasons. Things at the hospital happened so fast that I was convinced that this was destiny.

"I have been tough on Hatim but I do love him and respect him more than my own son. In my heart, I have never differentiated between Hatim and my other two children. But I guess there is a difference between your own blood and the blood of somebody else. Hatim never seems to understand me and is against me in everything I say and do. Have I made a mistake by taking him away from his family? I lied to my wife that he was our firstborn. Is this lie costing me my happiness? Is this the destiny I need to accept and live by? I may die with this secret and no one will ever know of this fact. I just hope that someday Hatim will come back to me as my first and own son as God knows the truth that I have always treated him as my own son."

The old Hatim would have had an emotional breakdown, but the new Hatim was proud of his father's act. His internal conversation was full of awe for his dad. This reinforced the fact that the assumptions he had carried about his dad were indeed like termites in his mind. Had he continued living with those assumptions, he would have lived like a perfect fool his entire life. He decided to keep his father's secret intact and work towards being a true son to him.

He flipped through the pages and the words 'great trial' caught his eye. He read the section.

"They have come to me asking for more money and they are not good people. If I don't pay, they will take away everything I have. I am under a great trial and don't know the way out. I have to meet them and convince them to leave me alone. I am broke, and I don't know how to pay this huge sum. Sometimes I feel like completely giving up and running away. But then how will my family ever face this problem? I haven't done anything wrong to anybody yet I am facing a mountain that I can't climb. God alone has to help me overcome this. I am tired and helpless waiting for some unseen help. Most important of all I should…"

The sentence ended abruptly. Hatim was not able to understand the situation his father was in. He had never given even the slightest hint about being in such a situation. Hatim sat on the floor. He couldn't control his tears. All this while, he had misunderstood his father. "I must turn around whatever he is undergoing and stand by him like a rock. Whatever is the case, nobody other than me should know anything," he told himself.

Hatim picked up the old telephone handset and dialed a number from his telephone book. "Fernandez," came the response. "Uncle, I am Hatim here. Mr Gawain's son." Fernandez took a minute and then responded, "Of course, I remember. How come you are calling me at this hour?" Hatim told him about his dad's absence from home and asked him if he knew anything. Fernandez answered in the negative. For the next hour and forty minutes, Hatim called all his father's friends and the response was the same. His mother served him dinner and sat beside him. There was an endless silence, which was broken by the phone ringing. Hatim jumped instantly and picked up the receiver.

The voice on the other end was very rough and abrupt. "You have thirty hours to get us four Lakh rupees or else you can forget your dad forever." Hatim closed the door behind him and said, "Hello, hello who is this? And how can I be sure that my dad is with you?" He then heard his dad's feeble voice on the other end. Hatim said, "Dad, I am Hatim here. Don't worry, I will get you out and nothing is going to happen, I promise." The rough voice repeated, "Thirty hours from this minute is all you have. Drop the money at the Paper Bazaar petrol bunk by 6 a.m. the day after."

Hatim shared minimum information with his mother and sister. He told them that his dad owed someone money and they were asking for it to be returned. He also said that he would organize the money and get his father back home soon.

Hatim took his father's bike and left at 11 p.m. He remembered the night he walked out on his dad. He went straight to Chandy's house and knocked the door. He was greeted by Chandy's mom who was a real sweetheart. Chandy was pretty surprised to see Hatim. Hatim explained to him briefly what the situation was. It was going to be a long hectic night. Chandy took his parents' permission and went out with Hatim. "People are my greatest resource," a voice echoed in his mind. They went straight to Jasbir's house for a loan.

Jasbir was a well-known moneylender and Hatim was sure he would help. Jasbir spelt out the interest rate and Hatim had no choice but to accept it. Chandy stood guarantee for the loan. Hatim hated this moment but there was no other way out. Jasbir said the money would be ready the following day by 5 p.m. as the currency was in transit.

Back home, both Hatim's mother and sister slept out of exhaustion and partial relief. Hatim sat beside them and just looked at them for a while before he hit the sack.

Chapter 17

War

War does not determine who is right, only who is left.

- George Bernard Shaw

Hatim woke up early and offered his prayers. For the first time in his life, his prayer seemed very different. It was a profound experience of communicating with the one who had created him and given him the intellect, understanding, capability, realization and guidance to transform. Hatim was completely tuned to who he was, where he was and where he was heading in life. An immense feeling of gratitude overwhelmed his thoughts and emotions. This feeling replaced the usual list of expectations he ritually mumbled in his prayers. The expression of gratitude in his prayers gave him inner strength and a conviction that piety and righteousness would always conquer any evil he had to face.

Hatim picked up his father's paraphernalia once again. With patience, he browsed through the various documents and diaries. On the last page of his personal diary, at the bottom was written, in very tiny letters, the name 'Rudra', along with a phone number. According to his mother, the last call that had come in before his father left home was from Rudra. Hatim feared going to the police due to obvious reasons. He had a quick breakfast and rushed out telling his mom that he would be back by evening and they did not have to wait for him at lunch. He headed straight to the telephone billing center and spoke to the rather lethargic-looking front office guy.

"Sir, I need the address of one Mr Rudra who owns this number." He handed over the small chit that contained Rudra's number. When he dialed the number, the call wouldn't go through. The front office executive wanted to know what the issue was. Hatim explained that Rudra could help him find his missing father. Minutes later, the address was with him. It was a good twenty-minute ride to Rudra's place. It was a posh bungalow with a guard at the main gate. "*Rudra sab se milna hai* (I am here to meet Mr Rudra)," he said and the guard asked him if he had an appointment. Hatim replied in the negative. The guard picked up the intercom and explained Hatim's presence at the gate. He was ushered into the bungalow, which looked rather deserted. He was made to sit in the informal hall. A frail-looking servant brought him a glass of fresh pineapple juice. Sipping the juice, Hatim waited for Rudra. A few minutes later, a short stubby man in his late fifties, with a very laidback attitude walked into the hall. "Rudra," he said pointing at his belly. He was sort of giggling. "Good morning, sir. I am Hatim, Gawain's son." "I know, I know you very well, probably better than you know your own self," Rudra said and chuckled again.

Before Hatim could begin his next sentence, Rudra continued, "I told your dad not to get into this mess but he wouldn't listen." Hatim was clueless and that was pretty evident on his face. Rudra slumped into the heavy sofa with a thud and said, "I just asked him to sign on the property papers and he refused. This property is a very important piece of land for a big project coming up on the ring road. We agreed to pay him a price. But he was adamant saying that this land belonged to the family and he was not willing to sell it. We have other methods to get what we want, you know."

Hatim was losing his patience. He stood up and nearly shouted, "What did you do to my dad?" Rudra chuckled and said, "I have not started yet, my boy"

Hatim was feeling disoriented. As he fell back into the sofa, he wondered if the juice he had had a few minutes ago was poisoned.

Chapter 18

A Bulletproof Mind

Knowledge is knowing that tomato is a fruit, wisdom is not adding it to a fruit salad.

- Anonymous

Hatim woke up with a very bad headache. He was in a small dark room with minimal ventilation and a strong cigarette odor. The flooring was ancient and there were tires and automobile spares all over. There was a table with a water bottle. He took a few minutes to gather what had transpired over the last few hours. He looked at his watch and it showed 11.30 a.m. He had to deliver the cash by the next morning to get his father out of danger and here he was stuck in this mess. He was not able to put the whole puzzle together. The caller demanded four Lakhs and Rudra was asking for land. Were these two the same people? Or were there different angles to the story? He called out through a small opening in the door. A brawny man unlocked the door. He was followed by four more thugs and finally Rudra. They made Hatim sit on a chair and offered him tea. Rudra chuckled and said, "No drug in this." Hatim drank all the water from the bottle on the table without asking for permission. Had he been the old Hatim, he would have panicked and palpitated. But with what had happened to him over the last week, Hatim was ready for war. He was a complete warrior now, ready to take on any challenge that came his way. He sipped the tea and asked, "I want to see my father now."

Rudra smiled and said, "You mean Mr Gawain? I thought you gave up on him and walked out of his house. From where did you get these noble feelings for him now? When he was in a mess, you were not around to help. Today I need his signature and you people have hidden him from me. I will get him at any cost because I am really good at hunting mice in the dark. I will hold you as bait and your dad will come to me by himself and sign the papers."

Hatim was not affected by Rudra's loose talk. A strong statement repeated in his mind. "The meaning of my communication lies in the response." He calmly began, "I have no clue what you are talking about. If you want me to cooperate and be of some use, you will have to give me more details."

Rudra had a wicked smile. "Your dad owns half an acre land in the north of the city, which falls exactly between two chunks of land that my client had purchased. My client needs your father's piece of land to make it a single property, which will be ideal to develop into a state-of-the-art residential township. Your father is stubborn and does not want to let go of the land. My client is willing to pay some compensation for it."

Hatim interjected, "What do you mean by some compensation?" Rudra chuckled again, "You have grown up *eh*, Hatim? We were ready to give him ten Lakhs for it." Hatim said, "You offer peanuts and expect my dad to agree. Your client seems to be a stupid penny-wise-pound-foolish businessman." Rudra was visibly angry as his eyebrows twisted but he chuckled again, "I don't get carried away easily, Hatim. All I want is your dad's signature. Where can I find him?"

It was clear that the people who had called him for the ransom were not Rudra's men. Hatim realized that his father being kidnapped was a sort of blessing in disguise.

The question Hatim asked himself now was, "How can I breakthrough both the situations with a single blow? What is the best choice I can make in this situation that can be the best solution for everyone? How can I ensure my dad does not lose any money and is released from the clutches of the people who are holding him?"

After a long pause, Hatim continued, "Indeed you got it right. My dad is stubborn and can do anything but only if he wishes so. He doesn't fear his own death or me being held here. But one thing is for sure, he will never compromise on his principles. I have always had problems with him and I hate this attitude of his. That's why I walked out of his life." Rudra sensed an opportunity here and asked, "Then why are you back?" Hatim responded immediately, "I have come back to take my share that I am entitled to get and I am confident I will do whatever it takes to make this happen."

Rudra took Hatim by his arm and walked out of the room into a plush office. Closing the doors behind him, he said, "Now let us talk business." Hatim felt a flutter of success within him, which he concealed well. Hatim was in charge now and he took a spontaneous lead. "What are you getting out of the whole deal?" he asked Rudra.

Rudra was destabilized by this question but replied, "What does that have to do with you?" Hatim firmly said, "It is all business. You want to make more out of the deal, right?" Rudra couldn't help but nod in the affirmative. Hatim continued, "If you can be absolutely transparent, we can both make much more without any problem and without playing dirty." Rudra said, "They are paying me one percent of the entire deal." Hatim whispered, "Peanuts." He made sure Rudra heard it. But Rudra pretended that he didn't hear anything. Hatim led again, "I will ensure you get double if you do exactly as I say." Rudra had no choice, he just nodded. Hatim said, "Rudra, can you indicate what is the current market price of my dad's land?" Rudra said, "About eight-and-a-half crore rupees." Hatim was shocked to hear this but he did not allow himself to get overwhelmed and react. He picked up a calculator and started thinking aloud, "Hmm…eight-and-a-half divided among the five people at home, so each person's share is about one crore seventy lakhs. If I take two percent of the eight-and-a-half crores, it comes to seventeen lakhs for Rudra. I will need about ten lakhs to start convincing my dad now. Rudra, but why were you were offering dad just ten lakhs?"

Rudra was stumped and replied, "Errr… Actually my client offered sixty lakhs as your dad's papers were not complete. And honestly, I was being smart." Hatim looked straight into Rudra's eyes and said, "I appreciate your honesty and I don't want you to lose a penny in this deal. Tell me, what will make you comfortable?" Rudra said, "Sir, I will be happy with forty lakhs."

Hatim said, "Done! And now here is the plan. You will tell your client that my dad has agreed for a joint venture where he will be a partner in the project with the property papers in complete compliance. He will be entitled to a fifty percent share on the constructed area of his land and a down payment of sixty lakhs in cash. These are the minimum terms to convince him to join hands. Or else, it will be difficult for him to agree."

Rudra said, "I am not sure this will work."

Hatim was unconsciously contemplating in his mind, "People respond to their representation of reality, not reality itself."

Hatim said, "Rudra, the other danger is dad could jeopardize the project with his stupidity by applying for a legal stay as most of his advisors are lawyers. You are the only one who can make this happen and you must convince your client about this proposal. Once there is a stay in the place, your client will have to cough up more and the project can get delayed. Most importantly, you and I get nothing at the end of this ordeal. I am sure you are not the one who enjoys fighting and getting nothing at the end of the deal. You are a businessman and a smart businessman, I assume. My proposal is a win-win-win for your client, you and my dad. And yes, you will have to get an advance of ten lakhs by this evening for me to convince dad."

Every sentence Hatim spoke was tailored. It was as though Naada was tutoring him to use the power of vocabulary hidden in a warrior. Hatim realized the power of being a 'warrior within' as he went through this transaction using words, visuals, questions, beliefs, opinions and assumptions. Rudra still looked at Hatim with uncertainty. Hatim stood up and walked back to the room where he was locked and sat on the chair. "I will wait here till you return and I mean business." This act of Hatim was the final nail in the coffin as Rudra was now completely convinced with Hatim's attitude. Rudra picked up his coat and quickly walked out of his office towards the Montreal Builders' office.

Chapter 19

A True Warrior

Have a strong mind and a soft heart.

- Anthony J. D'Angelo

Rudra was gone for almost three hours. Hatim was now being treated with much more respect in the dingy room. He was served snacks and allowed to make calls. He called his mother and comforted her. He repeatedly instructed to her that if she received any calls, she must not divulge any information but instead ask the caller to call back after 7 p.m. He called Chandy and asked him to inform Jasbir that they would be late. Chandy sounded very concerned and asked repeatedly if everything was fine. Hatim assured him that everything was in control and did not divulge any details. He told himself, "I must take the ship to the shores through calm waters. I must not get excited, but hold tight to my stand of resolving both the issues." He looked up to the heavens and made a silent prayer.

The phone rang and it was Rudra. Hatim was a bit uneasy as he had expected Rudra to return by now with the cash. Rudra spoke. "Hatim, I had a detailed discussion and my client is ready to pay even one crore but he is willing to give only forty percent of the built-up area as your dad's share." Hatim did not respond for a while and Rudra called out aloud, "Hello." Hatim then said, "Please give me a few minutes and call back."

Three minutes later, Rudra called back. Hatim proposed the client give eighty lakhs non-refundable cash and a forty-five percent area as his father's share. He was put on hold. A minute later, Rudra's enthusiastic voice came back with a confirmation. Hatim casually said, "I need ten lakhs today to be able to convince my dad." Rudra said, "I already have it with me." Hatim was smelling victory in the air.

About thirty minutes later, Rudra handed over ten lakhs to Hatim and they parted ways, promising to meet again the next evening for the finalization of the deal. Hatim headed home and deposited the money in the safety vault. He called Chandy and informed him that he had arranged the money through an alternative source, which didn't require him to pay interest. He asked Chandy to call Jasbir to hold the loan. Chandy asked Hatim if everything was fine and if he needed any help. Hatim reiterated that everything was in control and they could meet later that night.

Hatim sat by his mother and sister waiting for the call. At 9.05 p.m., the phone rang. It was Rudra. He informed Hatim that the joint venture papers were being prepared and he could see the draft by noon the next day. Rudra cautioned Hatim that this was one appointment he must not miss. Hatim had expressed his interest to meet the builders who were to develop the project and Rudra had agreed to it.

Hatim told his mother and sister to move to the bedroom and lock it. He told them that he was expecting an important business call. The next call was at 9.40 p.m. It was the same rough voice again. "Have you organized the money?" Hatim replied with a firm "yes." The voice seemed a bit familiar now. Hatim was trying to figure out who it could be but he wasn't able to put a face to the voice. "Put the money in a black plastic cover and throw it in the dustbin at the petrol bunk in Paper Bazaar." Hatim now responded, "I have the money with me right now, but I will hand it over to you in person once I see my dad." The caller's voice turned restless. "I want you to do exactly as I say." But Hatim was equally tough and replied like a broken record, "I have the money with me right now, but I will hand it over to you in person once I see my dad. I have not informed the police, I have not informed anyone yet. All I want is my dad and the property papers." The last bit of the statement was like a sharp arrow that shot through the phone. The rough voice changed momentarily to a completely different tone, "Err... which papers? What are you talking about?" Hatim sensed a cue in the voice and the accent, especially the manner in which he had pronounced the word 'talking.' He was certain now who it was. Hatim said in a stern voice, "Chandy, cut the rubbish and let us get this straight and over." The phone hung up. Hatim looked at his watch and waited.

It rang in the next minute. He heard a sob and it was clearly Chandy. "I did it to protect uncle and I never knew it would get so dirty." Hatim replied calmly, "We all make mistakes Chandy and I am willing to listen." In the back of Hatim's mind rang the sentence, "People always make the best choice available to them."

"Where can I pick you and my dad from?"

"We are right behind the Ganga Circle Bakery in a small house with blue tiles." Hatim said, "Chandy, I want you to meet me at the bakery first before we meet dad. I don't want anyone to know of your involvement in whatever has transpired." Hatim could hear a sigh of relief in Chandy's voice.

Chandy was completely shaken and didn't have the guts to meet Hatim in his eyes. "What pushed you to do this, Chandy?" asked Hatim. Chandy said, "My mom isn't keeping well and her medical bills were unaffordable by me. I fell for the fifty percent money offered by your uncle, Setanu. Knowing that you had left home, he wanted the property documents so that he could harass your dad into giving more money to him."

Hatim asked, "Where is dad and where are the papers?" Chandy pointed to the room behind. Hatim said, "Apart from us, no one ever in this world will know what had happened. And I wish to meet my dad now." Chandy led Hatim into the small house. Hatim saw his father sleeping in the corner of the hall, looking frail, helpless, cold and hopeless. "*Baba*," he said aloud and Mr Gawain looked up in confusion. Hatim rushed forward and hugged his father like never before. He cried and uttered words he had never spoken before. His father was unable to control his tears and wept. He repeatedly said, "How could you leave me and go away?" It took them almost ten minutes to return to a normal state. They hugged again and again. Hatim kissed his father on the forehead and said, "I belong to you, *baba*. That is the truth and I promise I will stand by your side till death do us apart."

All misunderstanding and assumptions seemed to fade away that minute. Chandy watched as tears rolled down his eyes. He was unable to believe the transformation in Hatim's personality. He was not the same Hatim who had left the city a week ago.

Hatim and his father took a taxi back home. They were given a grand welcome. There were no sweets and or new clothes but this was the best day of Hatim's life. While everyone laughed and cried, Hatim smiled. Hatim had turned from a boy to a man to a warrior. He looked at his folks and felt that he had the world with him. He looked at the skies and was immensely grateful to the one who controlled his destiny and the destiny of mankind. He remembered Naada and prayed for her wellbeing.

Once his father and family settled down, Hatim took his father aside and asked him about the property papers. His father explained to him that it was an ancestral property, which had five shares; two shares each for the two brothers and one share for his sister. He had paid and purchased all the shares from his siblings. However, his brother Setanu, who had already taken the money from him for his two shares in the property, hadn't signed on the papers. Hence, the property could neither be sold or built upon for the last fifteen years. He had left the house that fateful night to meet Setanu and request him to sign the papers, when he was kidnapped and locked in the house. Hatim asked his father if he could take up the issue and handle it to make business sense. His father agreed. He was more than happy to see a mature and responsible attitude in Hatim, something he had never seen before. Even his mother and sister were shocked to see the manner in which Hatim behaved with his father. They were pleasantly surprised to see the overall transformation in Hatim.

Hatim took Chandy and mounted the bike with the property papers and the black plastic bag. Seeing Hatim and Chandy together, Setanu almost lost his voice. He pretended to behave in a cordial manner and invited them inside his house. Hatim was not there to waste time. He began, "I wish privacy and no disturbance for the next twenty minutes." All the women of the household moved out quietly, leaving Setanu with Hatim and Chandy.

"I was heading to the police station with Chandy to file a complaint of kidnapping and attempted murder. I believe the punishment is more rigorous in cases where blood relatives and ancestral property are involved. However, I know that you have taken care of us in our childhood. My dad has always taught me to ignore the ninety-nine wrongs that a person commits and look at the one good deed he does. I have always exercised this value taught by my father. That is why I turned away from the direction of the police station and came towards your house. I want you to relinquish complete rights over my father's property. I also understand that you committed wrong because of your circumstances. I assume your needs drove you to do so. I understand the pain you have. You worry about your three daughters and their future. This is the four lakhs you asked as ransom. I give it to you as a gift. I will ensure that nobody comes to know about what happened and I expect the same from you. Sign the property papers now."

Setanu was dumbfounded and signed all the papers mechanically. Hatim shook hands with him and stood up. Setanu fell at his feet crying. Hatim lifted him and patted his shoulder. He walked away as Chandy followed him. They reached Chandy's house and Hatim looked into his eyes for a long time. "Chandy, you are one of my best friends and will remain so. This is for your mother who has always treated me as her son and shared pure love and concern for me." He gave Chandy a cover containing two lakhs. "Also, I need a committed assistant in the construction business that I am about to begin. I hope you are interested." Chandy was in tears but smiled and nodded in the affirmative.

The next day, the joint venture between Montreal Builders and his father was sealed. Rudra was happy, the builders were thrilled and his father was awestruck with what his son had done. The struggles of all his life seemed to have vanished. He was allotted twenty flats in the project worth over ten crores. His son, who was once written off, turned out to be the hero of his life. He said to himself, "I picked him with a pure heart and a pure heart is what I got in return."

EPILOGUE

Hatim is now a successful serial social entrepreneur married to Naada who works along with him. The entire family shares a common vision of making a difference to many lives. They have clear goals that align to their vision in life and are guided by strong values. Naada still remains Hatim's best coach.

Realizing the warrior within you is not an outcome of bestowed intelligence, formal knowledge or an acquired skill. It is the sum total of one's attitude that recognizes the truth within any knowledge. It comes to us as a predestined provision. Like a disciple, the soul accepts this truth with humility and gratitude. Once convinced by the truth and knowledge that surrounds it, the entire being surges forth in experiencing the power that life brings in. Unqualified and unassuming warriors are thus born. They turn adversities into victories and potential into opportunities.

Naada and Hatim live as simple warriors within. How about you?

The Poem of A Warrior

When things go wrong, as they sometimes will,
When the road you are trudging seems all uphill,
When funds go low and debts are high,
And you want to smile, but you have to sigh,
Don't give up though the pace is slow,
You may succeed with another blow,
Often the struggler has given up,

When he might have captured the warriors cup,
And learned too late when the night came down,
How close he was to the golden crown,
Stop and look at things without a frown,
Success is failure turned upside down,
So stick to the fight when you are hardest hit,
It is when things seem worst that you MUST not quit.

- Anonymous

A FEW LAST WORDS OF GRATITUDE...

The greatest gifts you can give your children are the roots of responsibility and the wings of independence.

- Denis Waitley

All praises belong to the Almighty. I am grateful to my creator for gifting me with the simplest yet most terrific mother in the world. My mom gave me unlimited freedom to make mistakes and blunders. She may not have undergone formal schooling, but she has the wisdom and acumen of a Harvard grad. The above saying by Denis Waitley aptly suits her. Love you, mom!

My dad worked overtime to give me the best of everything he could. He is an untrained warrior within, fighting battles that life throws at him. I learnt from both my parents that success is not about being famous. Fame comes with status, possessions and wealth, but greatness comes to those who are simple and live to make a difference to others. I cannot thank my family enough for standing by my aggressive nature, paradigm shifts, unpredictable attitude and lateral thinking. I thank my wife Sabeha for being an unconditional pillar of support and the best critic of my bizarre and crazy thoughts. She is the one who helps me integrate my ideas with reality.

I also thank my brother Sadiq, who has been a good friend always, allowing me to be myself and accepting me the way I am. I am grateful to my sister Heena, who has always reinforced my confidence, making me feel like a superhero in spite of a million blunders. I thank my children Izhaan, Zayyan, Rayyan and Huda for smiling at me even when I frowned. They have been among my best teachers. I thank my friends from St Joseph's Boys school and college who stood by me in the assembly and in life too. I thank my engineering friends from M.S.R.I.T, who taught me how to be crazy.

A special mention about Daee Moait, a great teacher and mentor, who enabled my transformation to a large extent.

I am very grateful to the teams mPower, mPower Foundation, Breakthrough360, Life Bridge and Ants2GiAnts for giving me all that they had. Every individual who participated in our training programs is in some way responsible for this book. I acknowledge and appreciate Notion Publishers for accepting this project. A big 'thank you' to my readers for picking up this book up and reading it till the end.